Scarborough Town FC
THE FIRST CHAPTER

Chris Daniel

Blackline|Press

First published in 2011 by Blackline Press

ISBN 9780956323866

www.blacklinepress.com
Blackline Press, 15 Lister Road, IPSWICH IP1 5EQ
info@blacklinepress.com

Blackline|Press

Scarborough Town FC

THE FIRST CHAPTER

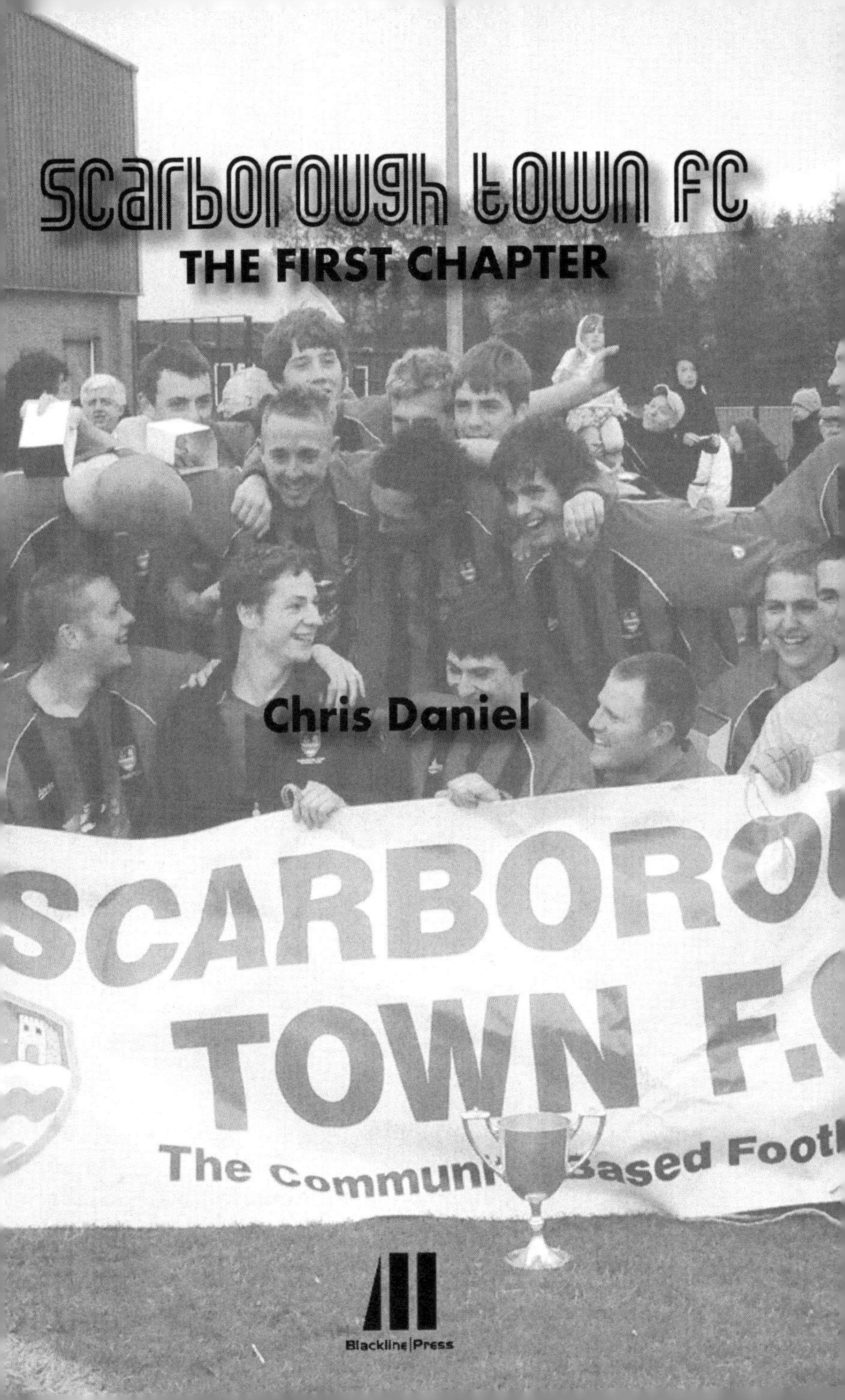

Chris Daniel

Blackline|Press

Foreword

For two years I was part of something special - Scarborough Town Football Club. This book intends to be a snapshot of those years, to convey to a wider audience the in's and out's, the tremendous highs and the depressingly low lows. What was so special was that this was pure football, stripped back from the glitz and glamour, away from the set way to play, where teams lined up in order to nullify each other. The book follows the journey of a team, with a simple aim of attempting to see how good they actually were.

It must be stressed that all the opinions in this book are my own and not the clubs, although it should become clear, this book is a celebration. The story does not have the happy ending that it deserves, but this is not a place for pointing the finger of blame, or theorising 'what if's' –this is about laying down facts for you, the reader, to draw your own conclusions. Whatever conclusions may be reached, just don't let it overshadow the on the field achievements of a group of best mates and their trials and tribulations playing the best game in the world.

Special thanks go to anyone who has helped in the preparation of this book, namely Hugh Bellamy and Derek Megginson for their information, Stuart Canvin for his brilliant photographs and to Charlie for putting up with me during the long hours it took to write this - it is greatly appreciated, however it is to Mitch Cook, Bob MacDonald, the team of coaches, and to everyone who pulled on the Town shirt – it is you that made this book – the memories and stories it provides, and as such, all I can say is 'thanks'.

2007-8

Saturday July 12, 2008 saw the beginning of a new chapter in Scarborough football. As Scarborough Town kicked off away at Hall Road Rangers in an early pre season friendly, a journey began. Well, the journey itself began many years ago, but Scarborough Town is the outlet through which the journey can be best viewed. Scarborough Town were far from an ordinary football club, and Scarborough is far from an ordinary football Town. Scarborough FC, with whom the author experienced the (some) highs and (many) lows were liquidated in the summer of 2007, ending 81 years of professional football in the Town.

The Scarborough FC Centre of Excellence and Under 19 team survived the closure of the club through the virtue of being rescued by George Pindar Community Sports College (GPCSC). GPCSC was already well regarded within the area – it had offered huge support to Scarborough FC during its final season, through sponsorship of matches, paying for coaches to transport children from the estate which its serves and their parents to attend matches they usually wouldn't be able to, boosting the crowds, atmosphere and burger bar takings, and through a direct link whereby one of the clubs players was employed by the school, raising the profile of both parties. GPCSC were part of the proposal to save the club. The clubs crippling debts were compounded by an ageing and expensive to run McCain Stadium. If the club could sell the site and move, as many clubs have now begun to do, to a new facility which could generate revenue 365 days a year, the club could survive. But the deal was blocked. Scarborough Borough Council would not lift a sporting covenant on the McCain stadium which would allow it to be sold to a developer to provide the funds for the new ground, and to pay off the debt. The Council claimed they were not convinced that this could work, or that perhaps the ground would go and nothing new be built. They thought a school, at the heart of its community, winner of the most improved school in the country one year later wasn't a good enough guarantee that this wasn't a developers get rich quick scheme.

Chairman Ian Scobbie had played his last hand. Despite the club breaking even for the first time in twenty years, without a move to a new Stadium, or the cast-iron promise of this to stave off the creditors, the largest being HSBC and HMRC, the club couldn't continue and were wound up. The McCain Stadium went into the hands of the receivers, who would spend over a year wrangling for its covenant to be lifted, in order to gain a higher price for it to satisfy the creditors.

This was not the end for football in the Town however, a new club, Scarborough Athletic were formed, but without facilities good enough for the league they wished to compete in, they chose to groundshare at Bridlington, a close to 40 miles round trip from Scarborough. Within Scarborough itself, the move of The Centre of Excellence and Under 19s to GPCSC, gave the impetus for long standing plans to be realised. Firstly, the youth system was extended to cover under 7s and under 8s, to compliment the already existing teams up to under 19s, under the new banner of 'Scarborough Academy' and Mitch Cook became Director of Community Sports at the college.

GPCSC is not your average school. The school has 'Trust Status' which essentially means it owns its own land and buildings – not the County Council, and has much more financial and management freedom. As such, it is the schools trustees which decide upon any course of action the school takes, and what it spends its money on rather than the Local Authorities. The schools trust board consists of representatives of Pindar PLC, one of the largest multi national companies to be based in Scarborough, through the Pindar family after which the school was named, and Sheffield United FC. The schools sporting facilities were good – with a leisure centre, tennis centre, skateboard park and full size floodlit Astroturf pitch, which was used almost nightly by the Academy, with so many different age groups training. With a desire and the vision to improve the schools facilities further, to be able to really make the school the hub, the centre of the sporting community, this was the place for the Academy

The 2007-8 season had seen The Under 19s, under the Scarborough Academy banner, continuing the membership in the Northern Under 19 Alliance East Division that they had previously held as the youth team of Scarborough FC. Still led by Mitch Cook and Bob MacDonald the under 19s were financed by those supporters, officials and followers of Scarborough FC who had an interest in the development of youth football – many of whom had been part of the former clubs supporters club.

The lack of a floodlit facility in Scarborough meant that the season kicked off with a 'home' game at Pickering Town's Mill Lane ground against Whitby Town's under 19 side. A Joe Danby hat trick and a strike from Neil Thomas gave the Academy a 4-2 win in front of a good crowd of 127. In ten years of Scarborough FC Under 19s playing in the FA Youth Cup at the McCain Stadium in Scarborough, no Under 19 game had attracted a crowd this large. The Academy finished the season with a record of P14 W8 D2 L4 PTS 26 and completed their fixtures top of the league, four points clear of Hall Road Rangers who still had two games to play, both against Harrogate Railway Athletic. The Railway postponed both matches, as they couldn't raise a team. This left the League Management Committee with a decision to make. They could award both games to Hall Road – giving them six points and the title, they could follow their earlier precedent where such games were awarded as a draw, handing the title to the Academy or they could expunge all Harrogate Railways results, which would mean the Academy lost four points, handing Hall Road Rangers the title on goal difference. On May 28, two full weeks after the Academy finished their fixtures, it was reported that Hall Road Rangers had been awarded the title. The Academy had no notification of this, and the League websites table still showed the Academy top, Selby Town second and Hall Road Rangers third. As Scarborough made this news public, within two days a new league table had been published – expunging all the results of Harrogate Railway as expected, but also all those of Bridlington Town, who had two outstanding fixtures, neither of which had any bearing on final league positions. The result was the Academy lost 10 points and ended the season in third place – remarkable considering that over a full season, in which both teams had completed 14 games; Scarborough finished two points clear of Selby, and that Hall Road Rangers had never topped the table at any point. Therefore, of the 8 competing teams, two finished pointless. As we will see later, it was not the last time the League Management Committee would make a decision which mystified those involved with Scarborough's participation in the league.

The Scarborough Academy, consisting previously of the Scarborough FC Centre of Excellence and the Under19 'youth' team had a rich history of success. Founded in 1988 under the instruction of first team manager Neil Warnock, who had guided the club into the Football League a year earlier, it was set up with a primary aim of producing quality home grown players. The 19 years it existed under Scarborough FC were nothing short of turbulent, but its success was clear for all to see. It was originally disbanded after just 5 seasons as part of cost cutting measure, but the reintroduced in 1996. Players constantly achieved the 'holy grail' of making the first team, then in the Football League, and later in the Conference. Ashley Lyth was transferred, after only 6 first team appearances, to Leicester City for £100,000 following Richard Jackson who had left for to Derby County for an initial £25,000. James Jowsey left the under 16s for Manchester United and Richard Crawford followed to the blue half of Manchester. Sean Rennison, David Pounder and Danny Brunton all 'graduated' to became first team regulars, with Alex Gildea, Paul Atkinson, Peter Fitzsimmons, Andrew Windross, Tom Raw and Graeme Carr all going onto make significant first team contributions aswell. Despite being dogged by financial strife, the centre of excellence in later years provided the first team with Chris Batchelor, Ryan Blott, Jimmy Beadle, Carl Cook and most notably Michael Coulson – who left Scarborough in the summer of 2006 for Championship bound Barnsley.

Scarborough Town FC were formed as an extension to the Academy side, to provide a club to continue the development of those players who reached the age of 19, and weren't yet 'ready' to make the grade at a higher level of football and would find themselves lost without a club resulting in them dropping back to the local leagues, and not realising their full potential. The club would offer senior representative football to the players at the Academy, and would give a somewhat more controlled entrance for many players in adult football – instead of being thrown into an adult team, they would be able to mature around players of similar ages who would be able to share the experience with them. The idea of an Under 21, or an Open-Age side had been talked about for some time. It was mid April 2008 when the idea became 'public'. Never had such a lowly ranked team caused such a stir. A statement was released through the school and a website was launched at www.scarboroughtown.net. Hugh Bellamy, the GPCSC headteacher at the time was to be the clubs first chairman, with Mitch Cook occupying a 'Director of Football' role. The statement quashed rumours which were circulating through the local area of a club to rival Scarborough Athletic, formed by those who had chosen not to support them, and reaffirmed the raision d'être of the club to;

"Provide a stepping stone to senior football for former under-19 players from the academy and community. The team will be made up of these players alongside a few senior players who will operate as player-coaches. It is intended that players from this team will continue to benefit from the coaching of the academy under the leadership of Mitch Cook and will be enabled to move on to play for a range of appropriate teams in the football pyramid, including Scarborough Athletic. The new team has not been established as a rival to Athletic and indeed there will continue to be a close working relationship between Sheffield United, Scarborough Athletic, George Pindar Community Sports College and Scarborough Town. All parties are committed to promoting football in the town and the academy's function is to provide a route for young footballers to achieve their footballing potential."

The club also confirmed that it had applied to the Teesside League Second Division – what was the highest level of football available to still be able to play at facilities within the Town. Tentative talk had been made about an application to the Wearside League, which sat two divisions higher, however this league would require something which would resemble much more of a football ground than was available in Scarborough at the time. Training began in earnest down on the beach in preparation, with as many as three sessions per week in order to be able to hit the ground running.

For many of the players, working under the tutelage of Mitch Cook was nothing new, with a network throughout the local schools and communities, players with the academy almost became a family, with Mitch continuing the work undertaken by his predecessor Ian Kerr. Joe Danby, Danny Jenkinson and Nathan Cook began playing the game together as 6 year olds. 10 years later, they were still together. Of course during this ten years, individually, their development as players was huge. But alongside this, they had also developed as the nucleus of a team. They had learnt to play football – not to get the ball as close to the opposition's goal as possible then hustle and hope. They had learnt to pass, to move, to keep possession and most importantly, how to play as a team. Scarborough is a relatively small place, but for years on the youth stage it had competed and more than held its own against cities, and football clubs of a higher standing, all because the youth system taught the boys how to play football. 1997/8 had seen the youth team embark on a memorable FA Youth Cup run. Home wins over Carlisle United and Hartlepool United led to the reward of a trip to the Reebok Stadium, and a Bolton Wanderers side featuring the now Premiership star Kevin Nolan. Boro won 2-1 – Stewart Morris scored twice. Morris would be another graduate from the youth team to play for the first team in the Conference. 2002 saw the youth team of Doncaster Rovers dispatched, with Richard Crawford scoring before his move to Manchester City, and 2005 saw the youth team crowned champions of the Northern Under 19 Alliance East Division.

At, coincidentally, Hall Road Rangers for the first ever outing of Scarborough Town, the composition of the team was entirely those who were either still a member of Scarborough Academy – namely Rob Clark, Darren Clough, Wayne Brooksby, Jamie Patterson, Robbie Hawkes, Nathan Cook, Sam Smart, Tom Hickin and Ged Dalton or those who had 'graduated' previously – Ryan Merron, Matt Perry, Joel Ramm, Mark Barber, Georgie Rose and Carl Cook - but found themselves drifting around local football, again not seemingly fulfilling the potential they had shown. The only exception to the rule was Marcus Jones – the 34 year old player coach. Jones was a former Scarborough FC player who still lived locally and as such was installed as the player coach to offer experience and guidance to the younger players – something they would surely need in what was, for many of the players, their first foray in adult football. The Rangers included two ex Scarborough FC players in their ranks, and played their football in the Northern Counties East League (NCEL) Premier Division, some 4 steps above that at which Town would be competing at. Although it is said to be naive to read too much into pre season friendlies, Town recorded an impressive 3-1 victory with Wayne Brooskby scoring twice, either side of a Joel Ramm penalty. By this time Town had been accepted to the Teesside League 2 division as one of seven new sides making up a 14 team division.

Another East Yorkshire side, Hutton Cranswick United were up next and although nobody would publicly admit it this would provide an interesting benchmark. Scarborough Athletic had drawn 4-4 with Cranswick recently so it would be interesting to see how the quality of Towns players compared to Athletics' NCEL standard side. Of course, again with it being pre season, changes were made a plenty, so the result of either of the games didn't actually mean anything. However, when Town came away with a 2-1 victory, the youngsters in the Town were beginning to demonstrate that perhaps they could play at a higher level and just needed the opportunity to do so. Town wanted to provide this, until it was clear that the players could play higher still, when a plethora of clubs within the region at various levels would be able to help the player compete at a higher level, from the Sheffield United link through GPCSC providing a Football League dream, to sides such as Whitby Town of the Northern Premier League (Evostick/Unibond or whatever glue you know it as), Pickering Town and Bridlington Town of the NCEL Premier and their tenants Scarborough Athletic of the division below.

For those who would follow Scarborough Town, this was a world of relatively unknown proportions. After 12 years of following a football league side and then 5 years in the Nationwide Conference, the supporters of Scarborough FC had it relatively good. By the time of relegation into the Conference, the gap between the Football League and below had shrunk immeasurably. Grounds and facilities were becoming ever so similar, as was the football on the pitch. Imposed relegation by the Conference through off the field financial issues had began to open an eye to a different world in the Conference North, with a transition from 'Stadiums' to grounds - furnished only with a stand and floodlights. Grounds which Scarborough FC had visited for friendlies were treated as a novelty, now they would be treated like Wembley! Tales of those who followed Scarborough Athletic were of park pitches surrounded by fencing, being able to drink beer whilst watching the match, walking around the whole ground and hugely outnumbering the home support – and that was Northern Counties East League Division 1 level, some 4 levels higher than the Teesside League Division 2 which Town would begin life in

August 2008

Before Towns debut season had even begun, two clubs signalled their title intent with huge first day victories:- Whinney Banks YCC gained an 8-0 away victory at Redcar Rugby Club, only to be bettered by South Bank St Peters who destroyed Teesside Athletic Reserves 10-1 away from home. Two scorelines that seemed so uncommon, if one of them occurred throughout the course of a whole season it would seem crazy! Town would begin the season with four away trips, as what was to be the clubs home pitch doubled up as a cricket ground throughout the summer, and so was unavailable until the end of August.

And so it began for Town, with an away trip to Teesside Athletic Reserves, based in Redcar. In the past, when Scarborough fans had watched their side playing against another teams second string it tended to be either be some pointless competition that didn't apparently warrant the first team, or that the opponents had their first team in a higher league. This was the case, as Teesside's first team were placed two divisions higher, in the Wearside League, boasting facilities of an enclosed ground - with pitch surrounds, dugouts and plans in place for floodlights, which would be needed if the club were to finish in a position for promotion. The reserves worked for Teesside – at a club of over 800 players, they were able to offer a full playing programme from 3 years old to adults. Last season's top scorer, Daniel Drazdukas, had moved up to the first team and would finish the season with 15 goals in the Wearside League. Facing the reserves however, Town saw no such luxuries as the first team facilities. The match was played on a nearby pitch, which was simply, a football pitch, nothing more, nothing less. Of course at this level no admittance was, or even could be charged. The officials were guys who didn't do it for the money, they had either done it for years or were young lads on the bottom rung just beginning the journey.

It didn't take long, the short pass and move disciplined, technical game was too much for the opponents and Robbie Hawkes took the honour of the Town's first goal after just 5 minutes. 6 minutes later centre midfielder Jamie Patterson, who had played with Hawkes for local league side Burniston, hit the second and Town were cruising. Two minutes after half time it became 3, when Patterson placed his second of the afternoon and became Town's very fledgling top scorer. Hawkes, not to be outdone, proceeded with two more of his own, to finish with not only the honour of Town's first competitive goal, but also Town's first hat trick. Rob Clark, not tested with a shot on target until the last 15 minutes, claimed Town's first clean sheet. 5-0 away from home – this was without a doubt a step into the unknown. Great Ayton United had the pleasure of hosting Town's second trip on the following Saturday. But again, all it did was highlight how different all this really was. For a start, kick off was an hour earlier than 'the norm' – and this was usual. No floodlights meant that you didn't take the risk of an early dark day. It looked like the sun was going to set with Town having played two, won one, lost one, but the side showed a bit of early resilience, as Josh Greening pounced with two minutes remaining to take a point back down the coast. It was nothing less than Town had deserved after creating plethora of chances

Redcar Rugby-Club-Football-Club were where Town were to visit next, which meant a second trip in three games to Redcar, and a second trip in three games to almost the same location, as the Rugby Club was opposite the home of Teesside Athletic. However the weather stepped in, and brought another unusual trait for those following Town – an August postponement due to a waterlogged pitch. You didn't get that back in the Conference days! So it was Acklam Steelworks where Town travelled next – a club that Scarborough FC had known all about. Well, not quite, but the two sides had met back in 1969 in a North Riding Senior Cup first round match up at the Athletic Ground. 1300 spectators had seen Scarborough run out 6-1 winners, the first step of what was to be Scarborough FC's 9th win of the trophy. Slightly less were at this match up – 1237 less if you are counting, as just 63 were present. This was Acklam's first season at this level, they moved up from the Stokesley and District League, in which they had finished second, behind Coulby Newham who had also made the step up. The season had started well for the home side – a 4-1 win over Coble Ennis Square had been followed up by a 4-2 win over previously unbeaten South Bank St Peters, so it was slightly less of a surprise when it was them who took the lead after 21 minutes following a fairly even end to end opening. Wayne Brooskby single handedly brought Town level after a mazy run, in what would become the first of countless Brooksby mazy runs, not just in the season, but in each game. Brooksby was an outlet – despite not possessing too much height and having a slender physique, when he ran with the ball it wasn't often that one man was able to take it off him, it took 2, 3 or even 4 to be able to stop him, which usually left 2, 3 or 4 team mates unmarked if he thought he couldn't go it alone. No one kept an official 'assists' record which was a shame for Brooksby as he would have probably been picking up the accolade. Just after the restart you could add one his to name as he cut the ball back for striker Neil Thomas to score his first in his first game of the season. Like Great Ayton though, there was to be late drama – after being comfortable in possession, but not scoring, Town conceded a free kick right on the 90 minute mark and were punished with a strike that isn't done justice in the Teesside League second division with only 63 people present. But Town were not to be out done in the late-scoring stakes, and attacked from kick off. Substitute Joe Danby, all of 16 years old, crossed, substitute Darren Clough, also 16 flicked and substitute Josh Greening – yes, 16 aswell, poked the ball home for a goal even later than his last. That was 2 goals in just 48 minutes combined of substitute appearances for Greening.

So it was back to Redcar Rugby for the rearranged tie and a thoroughly frustrating evening. It was a bad start as a deep, angled ball was not dealt with and finished after just 6 minutes. Town hit back ten minutes later through Robbie Hawkes, and should have gone on to take the lead but for a combination of good goalkeeping, wasteful finishing and not quite being in the right place at the right time, or simply poor positioning. Six corners in succession didn't bring a goal before the interval, but this didn't seem to affect Town as they came out for the second half in the same mood. Ten minutes in, they got their reward as another Brooksby solo goal gave Town the lead. This cued more of the former, when Town were coasting, as with the lead, things were less urgent and not finished. As it was, the Rugby boys hit back with an equaliser with just 8 minutes left on the clock. Town couldn't repeat the recent late shows and had to settle for a point. 8 points from the first four away games - probably two less than Town deserved – but football has a nasty way of not giving you what you deserve. Nevertheless, It was time for Town's first home game.

Grangetown Youth and Community Centre were the opponents for Town's first ever home fixture on August 30, for a real step into the unknown for the club. The four previous away fixtures had attracted crowds ranging from 82 to 48 – still fairly impressive figures for Step 9 football, but no one was able to predict what the crowd would be at the McCain sports field and whether people would be curious to see what the return of 'senior' football to the Town would look like. The day couldn't have been more different to what had turned out to be the last instance of home football in Scarborough – a 1-1 draw against Leigh RMI in the Conference North at the McCain Stadium. Now spectators could turn up two or three minutes before the 2pm kick off, no queuing at turnstiles, not even an entrance fee could be charged as the stadium had been replaced by a playing field, a roped off pitch with large PVC banners proclaiming 'Scarborough Town FC'. The club issued its first matchday programme – 'Talk of the Town' costing £1, a real labour of love, and worthy of gracing a much higher level. Buckets were passed around the gathered for donations towards the running costs of the day. For the first time it seemed people were conscious to what the money normally paid for admission was for. The club had to bring in enough money to pay for the officials, the food after the game and for the privilege of competing on the Sports Ground. The game itself ended with a 3-0 victory to Town in game when the scoreline flattered the away side and a victory of the double the margin would have reflected the game more fairly – so pretty similar to a couple of the games so far.

Perhaps it was appropriate that Town's first home goal was scored by Matt Perry – a player formerly on the books of Scarborough FC, the 21 year old hooking in after a parried effort. The response from a large proportion of people that day was the same – the result was largely unimportant – the day signalled the arrival of football back in the Town. The growing consciousness of the club was reflected off the field, sponsorship had been gained for both the playing strips, and 23 of the 24 starting eleven shirts had individual sponsors. The crowd was 223, dwarfing that of over half the FA Cup preliminary ties that day and even beating the attendance of two Conference South games – people in Scarborough wanted to see football!

September 2008

It was up to another reserve side just two days later for Town's first game under floodlights. The opposition Norton and Stockton Ancients Reserves, whose first team at the time played at Step 6 in the Northern League Division 2, boasted a fully enclosed ground complete with a new 160 seat stand, opened only 2 months previously, offering a somewhat different experience to the previous league games. As the season progressed, how those that were there would wish that this trip had have been saved for one of those bitterly cold winter games, as the luxury of having a roof over your head became one of the most longed for match day experiences. The game itself was far from a classic as Town recovered from a goal down to take all three points with Neil Thomas heading home Matt Perry's cross to win the game after Georgie Rose had cancelled out Chris Stockton's early strike for the home side. The result left Town sitting proudly at the top of the league that evening. It would only last for two days, as Wednesdays results saw Town down to third, with Coulby Newham and South Bank St Peters both gaining victories and continuing their unbeaten starts to the season.

Saturday September 6th saw the second postponement of the season due to weather already, and as such the McMillan Bowl (League Cup) tie with South Bank St Peters was pushed back 7 days. It was believed that the game would be a good benchmark as to where Town stood in the league. South Bank were regarded as one of the best teams in the division and like Town were undefeated themselves and more impressively had begun the season with four straight away from home victories (Acklam's victory over the Bankers was in doubt due to an illegible player). For the second game in succession, Town fell behind. 6 minutes had passed when Andrew Gove finished neatly giving the Bankers the lead. The short, fast, pass and move brand of football created Town many half chances, however it took until the stroke of half time for Town to equalise as Robbie Hawkes hammered home his fifth of the season from the edge of the penalty box. The second half was one way traffic. Town showed their superiority at playing football, their superior fitness and their discipline. South Bank's answer to stopping Town play was a series of ugly, nasty tackles to prevent Town gaining any type of momentum. 4 bookings in 12 minutes reinforced this stance. As usual, Wayne Brooskby was providing an abundance of tricks with speed, style and flair which, to be brutally honest, the Teesside League Second Division had never seen before. Another mazy run led to another crude foul, this time inside the penalty area, and Joel Ramm made no mistake from the spot. Brooksby then added a third to put the game beyond doubt and the last 25 minutes passed with Town creating a hatful of chances but failing to take them.

7 of the team who featured in the win had also helped the Under 19 side, known as Scarborough Academy, kick off their season during the week before the rearranged game. Away at the Under 19 side of Northern Counties East League side Pontefact Collieries, the Academy signalled that they were not about to be outshone by the newly formed Town side with a resounding 12-0 victory – the largest ever margin of victory in the division, in which goalkeeper Rob Clark converted a late penalty to finish the scoring.

Yet another game was cancelled the following week. Coble Ennis Square were due to come to Scarborough but after a tough start to the season it was unsure whether they would be able to fulfil the fixture. As the week progressed Town began to plan for the game as normal, the programme went to the printers, but an extremely low print run of 20 was ordered on the real off chance that the game would actually go ahead and to keep the blood thirsty programme hunters at bay – well someone paid over £9 on eBay to get their hands on a copy. On the Thursday, the game was cancelled leaving Town with their second Saturday off in three. Blank Saturdays, and no way of keeping up to date with the other latest scores in your league. How strange!

Free scoring Whinney Banks then came to face Town – with 9 points from their first 4 league games – their solitary defeat coming to South Bank St Peters, and a whopping 24 goals scored. It was here that it hit home how surreal football had become. We were slightly apprehensive about our team playing at home to a side, to give their full name, called Whinney Banks Youth and Community Centre. All eyes were on Danny Lockwood the Whinney Banks centre forward who had scored 25 goals in just 6 appearances. As would become a somewhat common occurrence, Town rose to the challenge with a display both exceeding their maturity and outplaying their opponents from the first whistle to the last. A healthy attendance of 139 saw Jamie Patterson nudge Town ahead after just 4 minutes, and Town dominate to lead 3-0 at half time. Any fear, worry or apprehension disappeared after the break and Town realised that there was no one they should worry about, as no team in this league could match Town if they played to their full potential. Add in the home 'crowd' factor – when a young, dynamic, skilful and fast moving side draw foul after foul, and Town's home advantage was huge. The goals flowed – Neil Thomas hit a hat trick, and Joel Ramm hit the ninth from the penalty spot with 15 minutes still to play. Ramm was lucky to get to take the penalty as goalkeeper Rob Clark, now with a thirst for scoring after his first for the under 19's, was well over the half way line after the award of the kick, trying to stake his claim. The result was the biggest league win by a Scarborough side since Stamford had conceded 11 without reply way back in December 1963 in a Midland League fixture, and that could have easily been beaten had Town not had a wasteful end to the match.

Two days later, history and reputation began to show as, through old contacts, an under 18 team was sent to Bottesford to tackle Grimsby Towns Under 18s – who included YTS players who were expected to gain professional contracts with the Football League side. The side including Neil Thomas, Darren Clough, Joe Danby and Nathan Cook, battled bravely to a 5-4 defeat, which included a rare missed penalty from Cook, and Thomas hitting the bar late on. The game just further highlighted the situation Town found themselves in. With a youth team and academy able to compete at the level that of professional clubs, the only outlet for them to be able to make the transition into adult football was in the Teesside League Division 2 – some 11 leagues below the first team of Grimsby Town!

Many of the players could easily have performed at a higher level at this stage in their careers, but being a unit was a huge reason that they played together. Many of the players had competed together and against each other since they were 8 years old. They had grown up becoming a team. If any of the younger players was put on his own in an alien situation, such as moving to another club, people failed to realise how much tougher it was for them. The simplest task of getting to training and matches becomes much harder when it's done alone or travelling with strangers and so some players did turn down approaches from other, higher positioned clubs – as they saw a potential to be playing at the same level soon enough, in a team they had grown up with, with huge forward momentum such was the vision of some of players at Town. They saw the club as able to provide them with the development they wanted, and the club was proud to provide that development and was thinking about how it could do more to help its players – despite only being in its infancy.

October 2008

October began smoothly for the club – Carl Cook, manager Mitch Cook's eldest son signed for the club as he returned from a spell in Australia. Carl had played for Scarborough FC in both the Conference and the Conference North and made his debut in a routine 2-0 victory over Redcar Rugby Club in the Alex Burness Plate (2nd Division trophy). The Plate would see Town play in a group stage along with 4 other sides, with the top two progressing to the semi finals. Avoiding the potentially tougher sides of South Bank St Peters, Whinney Banks and Coulby Newham (well, tougher going by the league table), it was expected that Town could progress to the knockout stages. Representative honours were to follow for five players, as Nathan Cook, Greening, Danby and Sam Smart made the North Riding Under 18 squad, with James Gunn making the under 16 equivalent. The under 19's won 2-1 away at Glasshoughton Welfare to continue their 100% start before Town faced St Mary's College. It took 85 minutes to break the deadlock, 40 minutes of these against ten men, but Joel Ramm fired home for another three points and another clean sheet. The game was marred by an injury to Wayne Brooksby after just 13 minutes, which saw him taken to hospital with ankle ligament damage. Perhaps this was another stage in the development of the team though – Brooksby was without a doubt the team's playmaker – from nothing he could create something usually by running, the ball glued to his feet, and without him it meant that someone else would have to step up and do that job. Another extremely healthy crowd of 130 attended the game and the reputation of Town was beginning to grow.

A tough trip to Teesside to face South Bank St Peters was next on the cards for Town. With both teams undefeated, Town were two points clear of their early title rivals. However the Bankers had two games in hand. If Town wanted to win the league this tricky away fixture almost became a must-win. It started badly. Town's earlier away results showed that although home wins were becoming the norm with larger crowds, which perhaps put a little more pressure on officials and a well manicured flat pitch, away from home things were different. Politely, the pitch was poor. Very, very poor. Far from flat, it undulated from goalmouth to goalmouth. The locals were aware of Towns growing reputation of fast, quick, nimble football. Away from home this unfairly meant that many tackles went unpunished as the lads needed to realise they were playing 'men's' football. If any of Towns followers dared to voice their opinion on an opposition tackle or a dubious refereeing decision, the locals would look, frown and stare menacingly. Should that Town follower still choose to defend his team, the men with the angry looking dogs would edge closer towards the Town contingent. As the locals intimidated anyone wearing the dark and light blue striped away kit so did the South Bank players on the pitch. Town, although dominant in possession, looked hesitant and slightly disjointed. As the second half began, with the score still goalless, South Bank sensed that further unsettling combined with a goal would break Town and for a while it looked like it may happen. South Bank took the lead after hesitancy in the Town backline, a goal greeted with an obese man somehow, incomprehensively hurdling the low rope barrier separating him from the touchline and breaking into a chorus of 'we are top of the league' goading the Town followers – namely the middle aged woman sat on a fold up chair, an off duty policeman and his young son, a young Scarborian couple watching a few friends, and a couple of businessmen committee members, proud to be representing their club, in their shirts and club ties. But the fat man sung too early. Cook had just sent Darren Clough on and he was beginning to warm to the game. With just 12 minutes remaining, he chased down a long ball and two defenders with a ten yard head start, before finding the far corner of the net for the equaliser. Within a minute of the restart, Clough produced almost an identical moment as he raced onto another through ball and beat the keeper. South Bank were broken. Jamie Patterson nipped in after a poor defensive header and sealed the three points in the 86th minute. Meanwhile, unpunished, one South Bank player found the most effective way of stopping Clough causing any more damage. Lifting him up by his neck, and pressing him up against a metal fence which ran a metre from the touchline, whilst the game was in play was a new method that hadn't been seen before. At the final whistle, the large gentleman was nowhere to be seen.

As the lads became accustomed to the Teesside League, it became clear that if this consistency could be maintained then Town would need to begin to look elsewhere to play their football next season – in order both to continue the players development and, for something which is unfortunately often mistaken for pure arrogance – to give the players a serious challenge week in, week out. The obvious progression routes were to look to the Teesside League Division 1 - which would be gained automatically through finishing in the top two places of Division 2 or the Wearside League – part of the National Football System, sitting at Step 7 on the football pyramid. Alternatively, the club could look to the Northern Counties East League Division 1 – Step 6 on the football pyramid, but with no 'official' Step 7 feeder league. Also at Step 6 was the Northern League division 2, however with the Wearside league an official feeder to it, the club would have to progress through this in order to reach Step 6 in this geographical area. Of course, the further up the football pyramid Town began to look, the more the ground requirements increased. The only league which would require no improvements would be the Teesside League Division 1. However, realistically, Town did not want to be competing in this league – as the season would show, the standard was not significantly better

After the Under 19s League Cup disappointment the season before, with a quarter final defeat at Field AFC, the trail began again with a home tie (well, at Pickering as usual) against Hall Road Rangers, minus crocked captain Brooksby. Jon Richardson, just 16 and old enough to be allowed to play in under 19 football hit four as Town cruised into round 2 with a 7-0 win. Now under 19 football is hard to judge, as of course you can be excellent one year then everyone becomes too old and you 'start again' so to speak the next season. However, considering that Hall Road were the defending league champions, and every single player who played that evening for Town would also be eligible to do so next season, things were beginning to look better and better.. If the first team developed at a rate which meant Town could no longer provide them with what they required, more and more youngsters were ready to step into the fold. A week or so later Richardson would hit another 2 goals for the Under 16s as they impressively brushed aside Leeds United's under 16s 4-1. Throughout the Academy, teams were recording impressive scores – regularly competing with the Academy teams of Football League sides. This was a true testament to the players – and a vision of how good they could be, and also, and importantly the coaches. The Academy received not a penny of funding and was healthily competing against sides receiving hundreds of thousands of pounds per season. All the Academy coaches under the guidance of head coach Cook were volunteers, and the hard work they put in could now be showcased through Scarborough Town.

After the St Marys game, many comments were made about the language, abuse and physical nature of the league so far. The statistics were resounding – already Town had seen over 30 players cautioned or sent off against them and had received only one single yellow card in return. It was a testament to the way the players had been taught to play the game. Mitch Cook was a huge believer in a no dissent approach – he was right – when has a referee ever changed his mind because the unhappy team have moaned at him? The Under 19s hadn't only performed well in the Northern Under 19 Alliance in the past, they had also won the Sportsmanship trophy in 2 of the last 3 seasons.

What had been a rollercoaster ride so far, but ultimately had not really had any disappointment, changed when Grangetown Boys Club, from the division above, made the trip down to the sports field. The competition was the North Riding Senior Cup, a competition which, like many county cups, struggled to have any importance for bigger clubs. Previously, at Scarborough FC, the competition was a distraction. Games against opponents such as Dormans FC, then of the Teesside League themselves, had been hugely inconvienient – opening the stadium for such games with all the costs that brought with it, were never met, as crowds barely reached the 300 mark. In Scarborough FC's last season, the two games 'Boro had played attracted just 168 and 185 respectively, in a season when the club averaged 912 spectators. This was reflected in the side 'Boro would field, as many of the first teamers were rested in favour of giving the fringe, reserve and youth players a chance. But this season it was different. Now Town were the bottom ranked team in the competition. Every team we could face would essentially be one of, if not our biggest, match ever. Grangetown BC were, along with Whitby based Fishburn Park, the next-lowest ranked opposition we could face being just one division above.

On a horribly windy and cold day, the game took time to settle and it was the visitors who went in at half time one goal up. Darren Clough was introduced, and had his usual impact, forcing the ball into the box after evading several tackles where Robbie Hawkes worked and finished his chance to level the tie. But it was unlucky 13 for Town, as with 77 minutes gone Darren Morrison's cross was caught by the wind and sailed over Rob Clark into the top corner. Town replied with a bombardment of possession in the last ten minutes, but couldn't grab an equaliser. A defeat. Crikey – what was that again? The Grangetown manager, who probably didn't normally give post match interviews to the opposing sides local press men said *'Scarborough Town are as good a side as any we have faced all season.'* The disappointment was huge though, despite Grangetown being the division above, people still thought it was a winnable tie and fancied the test against Northern League side Marske United (who incidentally, needed a penalty shoot out to overcome Grangetown in the next round before reaching the semi finals against a youthful Middlesbrough side). On a positive front, it did show the gap between the divisions wasn't big, on another day Town could have easily won the game. There was a brighter end to the month however, as previously mentioned, the under 16s travelled to Thorp Arch to face Leeds United and came back with a resounding 4-1 victory with Jon Richardson and Matty Brown, both of whom were just breaking into the under 19 set up, scoring along with striker Danny Glendinning, who was still actually an under 15 himself.

November 2008

45 minutes into November's first game and Town were well and truly having their resolve tested. 1-0 down for the second successive home game, this time it was Billingham Kader who had the lead, courtesy of Debo Babatunde an ex Liverpool Academy player. Darren Clough was introduced yet again, in the hope of changing Town's fortunes and yet again he did. Firstly, Neil Thomas was felled after work from Clough and Joel Ramm equalised from the spot. Then, within two minutes, Clough had worked his way into the box only to be met in the same way Thomas was. Ramm duly dispatched to give Town the lead. Not content with assisting, Clough had a change of attack from running down the wing, this time bamboozling his full back by cutting inside and placing the ball inside the top corner to put the game beyond Kader's reach. Both Patterson and Barber added to the score, as the one way second half became a contest of Town against Stuart Trotter in the Kader goal. The 45 minutes had restored Town's confidence, if they had indeed lost any. They had returned to their usual style -converting possession into making chances, and had taken a few of them, reaffirming their game dominance which wore and wore their opponents down almost pummelling them into submission with the nonstop approach.

It was when Town effectively used this approach that no other team could effectively match them. It started at the back, Rob Clark would always look short with his goal kicks – keeping possession rather than punting the ball towards the half way line, putting the outfield players in a physical confrontation they could easily lose. Whenever he claimed the ball in open play he would immediately be on the edge of his box looking for a throw, or a roll, to allow the opposition no rest. From corners Town would leave 3 men up – one on the half way line and two more on the opposite touchlines, wide. This left the opposition with a dilemma – either leave 4 men back – massively diminishing their chance of scoring, or overload and hope not to get caught on the break. Town wanted this to happen and with full faith in their defenders to be able to win the ball it often turned defence into attack. This fast, full action approach often led to the opposition committing many fouls, just to slow the game down and earn a rest, but Town won games by not letting this happen. Every free kick was quick to get the ball moving and to resume the rhythm. It was short, to keep possession rather than make it a lottery, and it was precise, creating opportunities whenever possible. A little more in the clinical department and Town could have looked at double figures a few times, but then again, a little more in the clinical department and the team wouldn't be together long – as hitting double figures every week would attract even more attention - not that this would be a major problem, with the calibre of the academy players who were yet to taste first team action.

Town's next game, the Second Round MacMillan bowl clash with Division 1 side Guisborough Quoit Club, showed a realistic opportunity for the progression to begin. Heavy rain left the McCain Sports Ground waterlogged however at GPCSC, where significant improvements had already been made to the playing surface in anticipation of Town moving there later in the season, the pitch was fit and the game went ahead at the 'new ground'. Again, this was simply a roped off football pitch but the possibilities for development were far greater than at the Sports Ground. With chairman Hugh Bellamy realising the importance that the football club could play in the local community and the positive impact it could have, it was the logical step to bring the senior side to the same place the Academy was based. The Quoit Club were no match for a rampant Town who, below-par, christened the new pitch with a thumping 7-2 victory. There were two more goals for Neil Thomas, and a first goal for the club for left back Dean Craig.

Two days later the Under 19 side dispatched Selby Town 3-1 at their exiled floodlit home in Pickering to progress to the Quarter Final of the League Cup in what would be their last game of the calendar year. The club, of course, were third-in-line to use the Mill Lane pitch, behind both Pickering Town and their own under 19 team, so bad weather meant protecting the pitch wherever possible, meaning that a hint of bad weather meant no game.

As if 7-2 wasn't an emphatic enough result in the last home game, next Town faced Billingham Town Reserves and finished up 9-1 victors. Billingham had headed to Scarborough as the divisions 'form team' having pipped Town to the 'team of the month' award but, just like the teams so far who had headed down with some sort of a reputation, Town had almost disgraced it. A cold afternoon had not deterred another impressive turnout of 131 – around ten times greater than the average of many games at this level. Neil Thomas scored early with his eighth of the season, but Billingham hit back, complacency and sloppiness allowing an unopposed run at goal which was finished well. From there on it was the Town show as last weeks 7 goals was surpassed with a Darren Clough hat trick in 16 second half minutes and another two from Neil Thomas to leave a fight to claim the match ball. The table changed however, as it transpired that Acklam Steelworks had fielded an ineligible player in their victory over South Bank back in August. Acklam were deducted the three points they had gained, but the League management committee also decided that the game should be replayed – giving South Bank an extra game in hand on Town, leaving them now 5 points behind, but with 2 games in hand.

Josh Greening had spared the blushes of Town recording a defeat in only their second ever competitive game back in August with an 88th minute equaliser up in the village of Great Ayton, bordering both the North York Moors and the suburbs of Middlesbrough, and as such a tough game was expected as they made the journey south for Town's second tie in the Alex Burness Plate. Beginning the match with a new player with higher pedigree in Ryan Davies, it seemed tougher still. Davies had turned out for Scarborough Athletic previously, but didn't fancy the travelling any more so had dropped to his local club. It wasn't quite the impact he would have hoped for, as Town hit double figures in just 54 minutes to run out 10-0 victors, with Robbie Hawkes hitting four himself - as 9-1 wasn't emphatic enough in the last home game. Town topped their group, with 6 points from two games, and a goal difference of +12!

It was mentioned at this game that Town were exploring the possibility of the Wearside League for next season. It was looking likely that Town would finish in a promotion position to Division 1 of the Teesside League, however it was clear that the standard wasn't *that* much different, and also the standard of refereeing definitely wouldn't be. Town could bypass the Teesside League's first division for the Wearside League, as entry was by application rather than promotion – anyone could apply, as Town had briefly explored in summer. Two obstacles stood between Town and Wearside football – a suitable ground, and convincing the leagues members to let them in.

December 2008

South Bank St Peters came to Pindar at the beginning of a bitterly cold December in a late switch from the McCain's sports ground which the groundsman had deemed unplayable. Despite catching some spectators out, the attendance still broke 3 figure as the league's top two, if not the league's best two, did battle. South Bank went into the tie one point ahead of Town but with a significantly inferior goal difference. But it nearly never happened however –the ground at Pindar was snow covered on the Friday morning, until Mitch Cook set out on a mission. Enlisting the help of his son Carl and Bob MacDonald the three began to clear the pitch, with help later in the day from Ryan Blott and Tony Hackworth, two of the footballers-cum-teaching assistants at GPCSC. An early Saturday morning inspection by Northern Premier League referee Steve Rowntree saw the ground passed as fit, only for the match referee to say otherwise when he arrived at 1.10pm (just 20 minutes before the game kicked off - turning up at that time you would think he didn't fancy it or something). After persuasion by both teams, and some well sourced sand, the pitch was deemed playable. Joel Ramm set the ball rolling early in a battle of football versus strength. The thing was South Bank were a half decent footballing side, if their manager had let them play that instead the result may have been closer. There was another for Robbie Hawkes, before two late goals as Town capitalised on South Bank being unable to keep the pace that the game had been played at for 70 minutes, and closed the game out for a comfortable 4-0 victory. A comfortable 4-0 victory against 2nd in the table – never had Scarborough's followers said that before! Yet again, for the fifth straight home game the supporters left thoroughly impressed, weaving through the myriad of materials by the entrance, ready for new building work the school was embarking upon – unfortunately not ground related. No one was sure whether the pile of builders sand was the same size as the one they had passed on the way in.

Town were beaten by the weather the following week, as the clash with Acklam Steelworks was postponed, but the week ended with Town receiving their first official accolade – picking up the Teesside League Second Division team of the month award for November after the 4 straight wins which yielded 31 goals. The hurt of the loss of the October award had been forgotten. Great Ayton United returned to Pindar the week after, wanting to forget their visit 3 weeks previously. That of course meant putting men behind the ball - which in turn meant that the game was forgettable. It took over an hour for Neil Thomas to put Town ahead, and Darren Clough sealed the points as he continued his own 'goal of the season' competition. This time hitting the top corner after cutting in from the touchline and evading two challenges. Perhaps more significant than the routine victory was the debut of another 16 year old, Matty Brown making his first appearance for the senior team with a 15 minute run out. Although Brown wouldn't see too much more first team action for the rest of the season, it signified his potential, and within a year he would regularly feature within the first team picture.

So 2008 closed what had been a successful beginning for Scarborough Town. Top of the league with just one cup defeat, 72 goals scored, with 14 conceded. Those following Town just weren't used to seeing such dominance of matches. The Town name was spreading. The future was looking bright – how high in the football pyramid could these players reach?

January 2009

The New Year started slowly for Town. The first match of the year was postponed, with Town due to travel to Billingham Town Reserves in the Alex Burness Plate followed by the home Macmillan Bowl quarter final the following Saturday also falling victim to the weather. This was rescheduled immediately for the following Saturday, which meant that Town were forced to cancel an intriguing friendly at AFC Emley of the NCEL Division 1 which had been arranged primarily to fill a blank week, but also to provide another benchmark. However, the year started much quicker for one graduate of the academy, as Ged Dalton hit the national media by scoring an injury time winning goal for Blyth Spartans in their FA Cup second round replay with Bournemouth, earning them a clash with Premier League Blackburn Rovers. Ged had lined up for Town in their first game at Hall Road whilst finalising his move from Carlisle United to Blyth, where he had gone following Scarborough's closure.

The Under 19 bandwagon was gaining momentum, with the side cruising into the semi finals of the league cup dispatching Bradford Park Avenue 5-2. Town players Danby, Clough, Brooksby and Greening (2) did the damage, putting the Scarborough youngsters into the semi finals for the first time. Senior football was paying dividends – as the players development was evident when they were back to face those of the same age. The fluency of the football was supplemented by the experience of physicality that the players now had – and this was beginning to become a devastating combination. Town finally kicked off the year the next week at home to Nunthorpe Athletic, who were having a far from spectacular season, but were from the division above. They had been beaten by Guisborough Quoit Club who Town confidently dispatched in the previous round, and as such, Town were confident of progressing. At half time, it seemed likely they would. Joel Ramm had fired the home side ahead, and despite only a single goal to show for it, Town were in control. The second half started in the same fashion, but the game changed instantly with the introduction of Darren Clough. Scythed down within a minute of his entrance, the referee, who could not cope with the burst of pace, was massively out of position. The loudest cry was a line of expletives followed by 'dive'. Clough was booked. Another minute later, as he breezed past his opponent with the ball, he was cruelly and intentionally scythed down again. Unhappy, he reacted to the tackle, which led to a coming together between the players. Luckily as this was right in front of the assistant he would be able to explain what had happened to the referee. But this assistant had history with Town already – with the pitch being adjacent to a hockey pitch, he had tendency to have a quick check to see what was going on over his shoulder whenever he heard a noise, regardless of what was happening on the pitch in front of him. Everyone sees things differently in football, or perhaps how they want to depending on what your thoughts and feelings are. Yellow card to Clough, and with it the dubious honour of Town's first ever red card – less than three minutes after coming on. Oh, and the referee was the same chap who had missed Clough being held up against the fence at South Bank a couple of months previously. More so, Clough had replaced centre back Tom Hickin in a reshuffle. Town down to ten, and had just taken off a centre back. Nunthorpe pressed and got a late reward pointing the game towards extra time, before Town's weakness at defending corners showed, and Nunthorpe had cruelly stolen it. Only the league and the divisional cup were left to win now.

A milestone was achieved in Scarborough the same week, as Scarborough Rugby Union FC opened their new £4million stadium on the northern outskirts of the town, to the envy of every football supporter. A project which had taken over 12 years to come to fruition, the club now boasted 4 full size and training pitches, including one with a stand and floodlights, a clubhouse with conference/hospitality rooms, gym and fitness suite – meaning that the club could raise significant money through its off the field activities. It was the kind of facility that Scarborough football longed for. By now, Scarborough Borough Council had purchased the Athletic Ground from the administrators, but its condition was dire – it was announced it would require up to £500,000 to be restored to a suitable level for football to be played there again, due to vandalism and no upkeep whatsoever. It was simply being left to rot. In the coming months, that restoration price would jump to closer to £1 million, and the council announced they favoured selling the site along with other leisure facilities in the town and replacing them with a new 'Sports Village' which would include a football facility. This could take up to five more years.

The following Saturday, it was up to the Middlesbrough estates for the first visit of the year to take on St Mary's College – a club not dissimilar to Town (well, they played at a college). Relishing the opportunity to host Town, College produced a programme worthy of a much higher league and were proud to proclaim it was their first ever – *"following the great hospitality and notable professional set up when we visited the seaside club in October, we thought as a mark of appreciation to provide our opposition with an official match programme to mark their first visit of the ex pro league club to the college"*. With a cover price of £1, it was a sell out, leading to a furious bidding war for a copy gracing eBay a few weeks later, with the lucky winner paying a small ransom for the publication. St Mary's were looking to avenge the narrow defeat back in October and were aided by yet another sloping, bumpy and massively uneven pitch for Town to face on their travels. Early goals settled the tie as a contest, and Town finished 4-1 victors, keeping the unbeaten league run going. St Mary's seemed more than content after selling over 100 programmes, giving a decent account of themselves and enjoying hosting Town.

The only team Town had not yet faced were Coulby Newham and after postponements and rearrangements the clubs finally met on the last day of January. Again, a healthy crowd of 115 graced Pindar with their presence, and those that did witnessed two more personal 'firsts' for players - Tom Hickin's first goal and Josh Greening's first hat trick, completed with a penalty, as Coulby were dispatched 5-1 for their heaviest defeat of the season.

February 2009

Yet again Town had another slow beginning to the month, as firstly the trip to Billingham Kader was postponed and the following week's trip to Norton and Stockton also fell victim to the weather. Both of these ties were due to be in the Alex Burness Plate, and despite Kader's valiant effort to get the game played – even attempting to switch it to an alternative venue – Town were stuck with just the two games played in the competition. During this time Carl Cook departed back to Australia, and as such missed the following week's trip back up to Kader – in a game which had been switched to a league clash as the league pondered what to do with all the outstanding divisional cup ties. Some football had kept half of the Town team match sharp, as the under 19s faced Selby Town at Pickering, and hit the net regularly again, this time a 7-3 scoreline being recorded as they continued their hot streak.

It is hard to describe where it was that Town faced Billingham Kader. Calling it a pitch would not convey what it actually was. It sloped in every different direction at different points, giving a rolling hill effect. Joe Danby will have been relieved when he got home and saw that the crowd of 37 was the second lowest ever at this point in a game involving Town, as not many people saw him head past Rob Clark to give Kader a shock lead. Town were on the ropes, with a team of flu ridden bodies and a pitch that meant the ball couldn't stay on the floor, the game was tough. Town needed inspiration; Donat Gomez gave it to them. Gomez was not Towns latest academy graduate, but Kader's 'imposing' centre back. Clumsily, he felled Josh Greening as he was travelling away from goal, but still in the penalty area, and Greening made no mistake from the spot. Not learning his lesson six minutes later, and still aggrieved at the earlier decision, he gave Greening another whack as he entered the box. Second penalty, second goal for Greening. Town went in 2-1 ahead. The second half saw Town try, but struggle, to get the ball down and moved quickly, but were rewarded with a third goal when Mark Barber struck from outside of the box and was aided with a deflection to wrap the points up. Not a classic again, but being able to win games on bad pitches and without the chance to play good football was all part of the players development, and so, another useful lesson was learnt.

Town's focus was changed slightly as the Teesside League made the decision to suspend the Alex Burness Plate and, its Division 1 equivalent, the Lou Moore Shield due to the volume of matches that had been postponed which, they thought, would take the pressure off completing the league season. Town were top of their group with two wins from two games and a +12 goal difference, and so were naturally disappointed that a realistic chance of silverware had disappeared without defeat. In the two competitions combined, 15 games had been played and were now pointless. Meanwhile, the competition for teams which had been knocked out of the main League Cup (Macmillan Bowl) in the first round continued.

Midweek saw the Under 19s score four against Pickering but only come away with a point. Despite not gaining a victory, in the coaches eyes, development and performance was more important and as such, this was a memorable week for the academy. James Gunn had made his under 19 debut and, along with fellow Under 16 player Ali Holmes, had also played on trial for Newcastle United Under 16s whilst Tom Chamberlain from the Under 13's spent time with the Sheffield United Academy. Off the field, Pindar showed its intent to enhance its growing reputation as a sports college by entering a planning application for floodlights on the grass pitch. For the college it would mean it could expand the community programme past 4 o clock in the evenings, as the floodlight Astroturf adjacent was heavily used, and the demand for more facilities was obvious. For Town it would mean that the club could possibly progress to the higher levels of football the team was showing it deserved a chance at.

The Teesside League representative side was picked for a friendly against Norton and Stockton Ancients in preparation for the upcoming National League Systems Cup. Regardless of being top of the second division, having defeated first division opposition in the cup and drawing growing acclaim, not a single Town player was called up, despite four other second division players being so. It was

mentioned it was because they were too young – well they had a point – we all know that you can't win anything with kids.
Liam Gildea had joined the Town ranks by the time Acklam Steelworks headed to Town. Having come through the centre of excellence along with his two brothers one of whom, Alex, would play Conference football for Scarborough, Liam also had experience with both Whitby Town and Conference North side Blyth Spartans. As such, Gildea would both boost the Town defence, and be a useful team mate for the younger players who could learn and draw on his experience as a young defender playing in the non league game. The game started slowly, and by half time Acklam had amassed four bookings as their strategy of stifling any fluent football worked. The second half began in the same vein, but finally one foul was inside the penalty box as Brooksby was sent tumbling. Josh Greening continued where he left off at Kader to give Town the lead. Joel Ramm squared with a quarter to go and Clough tapped in to make the game safer, then Ramm himself netted from close range with 5 minutes remaining to seal the victory in front of Town's lowest home crowd of the season, and what would become Town's lowest ever home crowd of 80. The game would also be notable as the last that Clough would play in a Town shirt, as he took the opportunity to move to Pickering Town, of the NCEL Premier, becoming the first player to move to a higher level after showcasing his talents through Town. It was working.

March 2009

Nathan Cook smashed the Under 19s to a 1-0 victory over Whitby Town, to take the team to 10 games unbeaten, in a testing game which served as an accurate prelude as to what the Saturday had in store for Town. Anthony Peacock gave Coulby Newham the lead after 5 minutes, launching the ball from 40 yards over the head of Rob Clark. Peacock was playing in the Teesside League with an impressive youth football CV that included both an FA Youth Cup winners and runners up medal with Middlesbrough. Peacock had encountered Scarborough football before, and is a curious case as part of Middlesbrough's side who visited the McCain Stadium for the final of the 2003-4 North Senior Cup Competition – what would be the 20th and final time that Scarborough FC lifted the trophy. Alongside Peacock that day included Lee Cattermole, David Wheater and David Graham – in a team that now has approximately 1000 combined Football league appearances, with Peacock being the only one of the starting eleven not in the professional game still.

Unlike that game at the McCain Stadium, Town today were playing at Kings Academy School, infamous as the first school in the UK to have CCTV in every classroom in order to protect teachers from harassment and intimidation. If only they were pointed on the pitch. After taking the lead, Coulby were quite happy with the one goal and proceeded to sit back and stop Town playing. Free kick after free kick led to the referee being constantly harassed – both teams felt aggrieved by a lack of decisions their way. Playing uphill and against the wind in the second half, Town's unbeaten league record was under its severest threat since the trip to South Bank in October. Town pushed, Liam Gildea became an emergency striker and added a more physical presence to the forward line to combat the defensive strength of the home side, and were rewarded as Neil Thomas found Gildea with just enough room to control and poke into the net with 5 minutes remaining. With South Bank on cup duty the result left Town 8 points ahead, but having played 2 games more.

With free weeks becoming more and more frequent and possible – a total of four teams had now resigned from the two divisions, and of course the Alex Burness Plate had been suspended, Town used the time to look to the future. A friendly was arranged away at Barton Town Old Boys of the NCEL First Division – the level which Town aspired to reach at some point in the future, and one it was thought was possible using the current crop of players. For the first time since pre season, Town travelled south, crossed the Humber Bridge and arrived at the impeccably tidy and smart Euronics Ground. It was exactly the type of ground that every football club wanting to improve would say 'something like Barton's would be nice'. Cover was provided behind the far end, 150 seats sat neatly in an arena-type stand at one side, with a large spacious clubhouse neatly in the corner. Part of the land the club owned has been sold to a housing developer, which in turn had allowed such improvements to take place. A new face pulled on the Town shirt as ex Scarborough, Hartlepool and Halifax centre back Denny Ingram wore number 5. Ingram was currently at Harrogate Town of the Conference North, but after a lengthy spell injured, playing for Town was ideal for both parties. Ingram needed game time to aid his comeback, and Town were short of a centre back, as neither Matt Perry or Tom Hickin were available, also, and perhaps most importantly for Town, what better way for young players to develop than by learning the game alongside one of the most respected ex-pros living in the town. With Ingram working at GPCSC also, making such an arrangement had been fairly straightforward. The pace of the game was frantic, Town shaded the opening half, but began to see what life would possibly be like at a higher level as Barton punished Town when Clark found himself in no man's land and was expertly lobbed for the Old Boys to take the lead. Not to be over awed or outclassed by their much higher level opponents, Town equalised in a completely unexpected fashion. Neil Thomas simply ran onto a long 'hoofed' clearance which travelled 60 yards in the air, beat the keeper to the ball and poked it past him to end the half level. Town started the second half brightly, and were rewarded as Mark Barber smashed a 25 yard effort off the underside crossbar, which the eagle-eyed assistant spotted had crossed the line to the delight of the travelling masses, who made up at least half of the 60 present. Barton hit back, and rattled the woodwork themselves. The game ebbed and flowed, with Town playing a significant part in an entertaining evenly matched game. What would have been a stand out result was soured in the sixth minute of injury time with Rob Clark pushing away a daisy cutter, only for the rebound to be tucked away with the last kick of the game. Still, a draw against a team from that level gave more credence still to the thoughts that Town were nearly ready to test themselves at a higher level – and that just the one level promotion would give, perhaps wouldn't be sufficient to fully stretch and test the players' week in week out.

Midweek saw the under 19s make the trip to West Yorkshire to Brighouse Town to face the youth team of Conference North outfit Farsley Celtic in the League Cup Semi Final. With the under19s able to boast a starting 11 of which 8 had first team experience, despite the away trip and the much higher standing of Celtic, the under 19s really fancied their chances. It transpired that they were right to do so. Semi Finals usually pit teams of quite similar standings together, something often represented in close scorelines . Not tonight, as the 7-1 victory booked the final date. A season that promised so much was beginning to shape for the under 19s, as they remained on course for a league and cup double. Meanwhile, it was confirmed that Town had applied to both the Wearside and North East Counties League's for next season, a decision where they would end up was not entirely in their own hands, so keeping as many avenues as possible open at this point was the logical step.

It became three draws in a row for Town when Norton and Stockton Ancients Reserves visited Pindar, and for the first game in their history, Town failed to hit the net. Off the pitch, the programme carried positive news, plans were in place in the close season to move the pitch away from Moor Lane by a few yards, to enable a permanent barrier and walkway to be put around it, and the club was confident of floodlights *'by the time the nights start drawing in'*. On the pitch the positive news dried up slightly, as Town huffed and puffed without the end product. At the end of the first 45, Rob Clark had barely touched the ball, and his lack of touches nearly came back to haunt Town, as with just ten minutes remaining, he misjudged a punch from a corner, with a miskick from 8 yards sparing Town conceding. Half chance after half chance came and went, and Norton's resolute game plan meant they became the first league side to leave Scarborough without defeat. Despite their lowly position, lying 8th from the 12 teams, Norton and Stockton twice against Town, had proved that they were no push over. With a young side, that attempted to play football, but also proved they could defend sternly when required, despite the massive disappointment amongst the homesters, credit was definitely due to the visitors. Pontefract Collieries under 19s bore some of this frustration as in midweek they were dispatched 10-3 to leave with a -19 goal difference from their two fixtures against the under 19s.

Following the under 19s in midweek, a big result again would further restore Town's self belief, and remind the league that Town weren't about to fall short now. Luckily, Grangetown YCC were up next, with just 1 win in 11, and a goal difference of -44 from just 15 matches. Unluckily, it was away. Grangetown has somewhat of a reputation of being a tough place – the BBC claim that the locals call it Beirut. Just 35 people, including the close to 30 travelling supporters, saw Town take to the field, which included a permanent barrier on which one could lean. A novelty not experienced in the league since the trip to Norton and Stockton in early September. The game saw Town's best away performance of the season, with a 7-0 victory boosting Town's goal difference even further. With the column taking even further significance due to Town being only 3 points ahead and having played a game more, South Bank's victory at Billingham Kader was pleasingly 'only' 5-0, extending Town's advantage to 16 goals. Town had slackened off significantly in a fixture which they could have easily reached double figures. A 16 goal advantage would hopefully be enough with only 4 games remaining for Town though, just in case it was wins all the way for both.

April 2009

Off the pitch things were as hectic as ever, as Town sought to further firm up plans for next season. The Northern Counties East League made a visit to GPCSC in early April, and left with Town very much still considered for entry, but also the stark reality that at present, the ground still had very few things in place which would be required to achieve the required ground grade. The Wearside League was a much more viable option, as it seemed that no hard and fast rule existed about Ground Gradings – some clubs had floodlights, others didn't, some had hard standing, others didn't, some had the entire ground railed off, some didn't. It seemed that if the club could get some improvements done – namely the pitch railed off, then this would be good enough for the league. From here, the club would need to be accepted by the other member clubs through a vote at its AGM in the summer. Of course, it was a significant step up, but the Wearside was just a slightly smaller step, and perhaps a better one for the players development.

Town only had 2 first team fixtures this month – with the first not being until the 18th, meaning the football fan's nightmare was occurring yet again – more free Saturdays! One of the free dates was significant though as Whinney Banks did Town a favour, defeating South Bank 3-2, meaning South Bank's game in hand had been wasted and they were still 3points behind. The Teesside League saw its third resignation from Division Two the same weekend, as Billingham Kader pulled out following their near neighbours Billingham Town Reserves earlier in the season– luckily this didn't affect the top of the table, as the top three sides had all taken six points from them. Town wise, it meant that Ramm, Greening and Barber all lost two goals apiece, and Joe Danby's own goal was removed from the record books. Expunging records and points adjustments in this way, it seemed were fairly common in this league, but were massively frustrating when trying to 'map out' the season

from who would take points where, and just as importantly, what the goal differences were!
Teesside Athletic Reserves then visited a jittery Town on April 18, who knew that all 3 points would put them within touching distance of the championship. 81 years previously, the town of Scarborough had seen one of its most important football games to date, as 6000 people – the second highest recorded crowd ever at this time in Scarborough - packed the Athletic Ground to see Scarborough FC face Scarborough Penguins as the two sides were both members of the Yorkshire League. The Penguins were still a club in its infancy, being only 6 years old, but had risen quickly to match and overtake the senior club, and earlier in the season had defeated Boro 3-1 in front of 6,600 – the highest recorded crowd at this time! Boro ended up following the Penguins lead in adopting professionalism, but finished lower than the Penguins in the Yorkshire League, despite winning the return 5-1. Taking the impetus from the crowds they had drawn though, Boro then moved into the Midland League, had immediate success and left the Penguins in their shadow, culminating in Boro absorbing the towns 'other' professional club just one year later in 1928. Although not quite on the same scale, for the majority of the 91 at Pindar, this was also an important day. With only one win in the last four games, and two complete weeks without a Town match, nerves were beginning to show, and facing a team who had been comprehensively beaten 5-0 on the opening day of the season, by a Town team who had hugely developed and improved over the season should have meant another comfortable victory. But no, Town made sure it was as hard as it could be! It took half an hour for Town to create their first clear goalscoring chance, Robbie Hawkes jinxed in the box, foul, penalty. Joel Ramm with 5 goals from five penalties looked on in horror as he saw his penalty saved. The nerves were creeping in. Still Town huffed and puffed, and the relief was clear for all to see when Neil Thomas poked Hawkes' low cross into the net on the stroke of half time. But within 5 minutes of the restart, the nerves had crept in further as once again, a corner was not dealt with and the Teessiders levelled through Jon Kirk. The crowd was expectant, and though Town were dominant the ball wouldn't go in.

Three defensive players in Ramm, Craig and Patterson (though they would all consider themselves able attackers!) were withdrawn for two of the 17 year olds in Josh Greening and Joe Danby, and a 16 year old in Matty Brown - all 3 having hit the net for the under 19s recently. Time disappeared, wave after wave was repelled - through resolute defending, a goalkeeper in Paul Orange having the game of his life (well, if it wasn't he was wasted at this level) and some wasteful finishing. As the game entered the 89 minute, Town had yet another corner, another effort on goal, another clearance, but this one fell to Joe Danby, who swivelled and smashed the ball across the face of the goal and into the far corner. He probably didn't see too much of the crowd celebrations as he found himself on the bottom of a pile of red and white, but the reaction said it all. To those watching Town, it didn't matter that this was the Teesside League Second Division, watching your team score a last minute goal meant utter jubilation. Then, as if the last 89 minutes had been easy, Robbie Hawkes found himself through on goal and firmly placed it past Orange to wrap up the game at 3-1. South Bank were not about to give up yet though, and showed less of the nerves that Town had as they put ten without reply past a luckless Grangetown YCC.

1 Scarborough Town	P18 PTS 46 GD +47
2 South Bank St Peters	P18 PTS 43 GD +29
3 Whinney Banks	P18 PTS 40 GD +35

First team affairs temporarily took a back seat during the week, as it was crunch time for the under 19s. At 'home' against Pickering Town, a point would secure the title for the first time since 2005, a time when the team included players who would go on to become professionals. Of course, when the two teams had met earlier in the season, it had taken an injury time goal just to get that point. Two hours later, trophy 1 out of 3 was secured. Darren Clough and Tom Hickin led the under 19s to a 2-1 victory, capping a memorable campaign in which they were still yet to be beaten, with a record of 13 wins and 2 draws.

Both the two Bankers' teams played their next fixtures midweek, upping the pressure on Town before they would even play. Two wins later saw the table tighten even further –

1 Scarborough Town P18 PTS 46 GD +47
2 South Bank St Peters P19 PTS 46 GD +30
3 Whinney Banks P 19 PTS 43 GD +37

So, for Town to have to travel to Whinney Banks, who only had 1 defeat in the last 10, and ready to avenge the 9-0 battering at Scarborough, the stakes could not be higher. This was without a doubt the biggest weekend in the clubs short history – as not only would Town play on the Saturday, but the Sunday saw the Under 19s cup final, which for some players meant 2 tough games in 2 days. Only Tom Hickin was rested from the last outing though, as Town began their assault on the perfect weekend. If this was to happen, much of it would probably depend on how Town coped with Danny Lockwood, who would end the campaign with a remarkable 47 goals for the Bankers. However, just as had happened when Whinney Banks came to Scarborough way back in September, Town showed no regard for reputation. For the second game against Town, Lockwood didn't get a sniff, and in turn that meant that Whinney Banks were in for a tough afternoon. A daisy covered pitch greeted Town at the same complex they had faced Billingham Kader, along with one man with two very vicious looking dogs, who placed himself just behind a nervous looking assistant, in case he in turn needed any help. A lack of goalmouth action meant the sides went in goalless, but Town always looked the better side, and it told when Neil Thomas did what he does best, got into position and tapped home yet another Hawkes cross. The weather turned nasty, and Town had two storms to contend with, but as the Bankers pressed, it left gaps. The physical side of the game increased, and every Town free kick was greeted with a volley of unrepeatable words, and a few barks. Town didn't take their chances as the clock ran down and entered injury time, but for all the pressure they had faced, they hadn't looked like conceding either. An injury time corner led to Whinney Banks filling the Town box, including a venture forward for goalkeeper Andrew Vickers. The corner was cleared and Josh Greening picked up the ball and ran towards the other the goal. Despite attention from defenders he calmly rolled the ball into the empty net to seal the points and effectively put Towns name on the 2nd division trophy. The storm had stopped, the sun was shining, the programme had survived. The Town followers left with grins which showed more teeth than the dogs.

It was back to Scarborough and rest for the six under 19s who had been involved, ready for the trip to the Claybourn Ground, Liversedge the following day. Yorkshire Amateur's under 19 side were tougher opponents than perhaps expected. Having 'The Army' emblazoned across their shirts was fairly apt. With a style of play that the first team had encountered all season, The 'Ammers' started strongly and mid way through the second half found themselves 2-1 up. As always, turning points came into play, and this time it was when the bar saved the under 19s from falling 3-1 behind. Instead, it led to a rallying cry. Town hadn't remained unbeaten all season to throw it away now. Darren Clough, who despite his first team move to Pickering still had seen his under 19 registration remain with Scarborough, as usual, used his pace to devastating effect. Nathan Cook kept his nerve to slot home a penalty with little more than 10 minutes remaining, and the under 19s felt it was there to be taken. The ball moved forward to Clough, his pace leaving the defenders unwilling to get too tight, so he hit it, low and hard from the edge of the box, across the keeper, turned, ran and was mobbed. The pile included Rob Clark who has sprinted a good 70 yards to join in, and the fact it happened in front of the opposition's bench was a just reminder that football can always triumph. Those who followed Scarborough football were used to by now seeing many new and different sights that the season had given them, but not many had come from the under 19s – cue Clough being grounded by a legitimate slide tackle, and then having the sand and dust of the end of season pitch thrown in his eyes to stop him recovering quickly. It threatened to spill over in injury time, as the 'Ammers attempts to take a corner were stopped by the referee who had bigger issues splitting a happy (and probably making sure his opponent knew so) Rob Clark and a frustrated opponent. A yellow card apiece, a corner cleared, and the full time whistle pierced the tense air. Job complete – 2 trophies in the bag. With Wayne Brooksby becoming too old at the end of the season to continue, the captain was able to sign off with both trophies the under 19s had been able to capture.

May 2009

For everyone involved, after the success of the past couple of weeks, May 2 couldn't arrive quickly enough. It was a chance to finish the job that had begun at Teesside Athletic Reserves back in August and lift the League championship to complete a brilliant treble. At Pindar preparations had been taking place for the big day with a bumper crowd expected to see the trophy lifted. Somewhat mystifyingly, the management committee of the Teesside Football League refused to travel to the match to present Town with the trophy, and furthermore, Town had to travel to Middlesbrough to pick up the trophy if they wanted to be able to lift it at all! The preparations were completed in time - the ground saw temporary boards placed down the length of the pitch, with seating placed upon it. Outside catering was called in for the first time, with a burger van providing refreshments and a PA system was set up. The opponents, Redcar Rugby Club, had no idea what they were about to face – the two previous meetings had yielded impressive performances from the visitors – a 2-2 draw in the reverse league fixture back in August, and the 2-0 Alex Burness Plate defeat in early October. It took 8 minutes for Mark Barber to open the scoring, and by the time Joe Danby hit the net in injury time Town had scored 12 without reply. Something they had threatened in almost every game had happened – Town had clinically taken their chances. The new record crowd of 235 knew they had seen something special. It may have 'only' been the Teesside Football League Second Division, but the manner in which the players systematically took apart their opponents showed what obvious ability the team had, and questions begun to circulate about how good this team actually was. Nathan Cook hit the goal of the game from 45 yards after spotting Redcar's luckless goalkeeper just a little too far off his line, outdoing an earlier equally impressive goal when Redcar failed to touch the ball from the restart before Wayne Brooskby slotted home. Town became the first side in the Teesside League to complete a league season unbeaten since Nunthorpe

Athletic in 1982/3, another nice touch that wouldn't be forgotten in a hurry.
Importantly, big plans were made public that day. A classroom was opened to display all the plans for the future development of the site – part the schools blueprint to creating a sporting academy that the region would be jealous of. Already on the same site an indoor tennis centre had been built, and with it had followed the relocation of Scarborough Tennis Club. The plans were grand, culminating in a proposal that would lead to a ground with 1020 seats, 510 down each side of the pitch, and small covered terraces behind each goal. Floodlights, turnstiles and hard standing surrounding the pitch were part of the plan, which it was also mooted could be a short term option to providing a home for Scarborough Athletic whilst the council promised facility was built. Short term the idea was for a stand of 102, with the floodlights and hard standing. As and when they were needed, the other seating blocks could be attached on to either side of the existing seats, giving a total of 510 each side. With the euphoria of the championship and the buzz of the idea of the pitch becoming more of a football ground, there was a feeling that the club was really going places, through its on the pitch performances and its off the pitch leadership and being part of the schools wider picture, which essentially supported the role that football played in its community.
The end of the day almost meant the end of the season, but one fixture was outstanding, and one small matter remained. The under 19s faced Whitby Town away, avoiding defeat would complete their unbeaten season. The job was completed as Nathan Cook dispatched another penalty, Greening and the returning Ged Dalton came off the bench to wrap up a 3-1 victory. It rounded off a good week for Nathan Cook, who at the clubs presentation night two days later took home the under 19's player of the season award with 8 goals from 16 games from someone who still had 2 more seasons playing at this age group. The Senior teams player of the year went to unsung, well not that unsung as his consistent contribution was massively recognised, Dean Craig, who had played in every single game, with the Scarborough Evening News' own player of the year award going

to Wayne Brooksby. Neil Thomas took home top goalscorer, with 20 goals, and Darren Clough and Joe Danby shared the under 19 equivalent. Finally, Rob Clark picked up the special achievement award, for an excellent season and the contributions he had made.

The Teesside League presentation night saw another accolade gained on the night Barcelona lifted the Champions League, as Wayne Brooksby was named runner up in the second division player of the season award. The vote was decided as after each game the opposition picked a man of the match which was then collated at the end of the season, The winner being the Whinney Banks goalgetter Danny Lockwood. The first division player of the season award that night at BEADS (or Birchwood, Easterside and District Social Club to give it its full name) went to a Fishburn Park player, who had come through the Scarborough FC School of Excellence, called Neil Waterfield, who, as a 6 foot plus centre back would be a nice addition to the Town back line.

Town's triumph and the Under 19 League and Cup double happened alongside a League championship for Scarborough Ladies FC and the North East Counties Division 1 title in flamboyant style with a NCEL Presidents cup final appearance for Scarborough Athletic. Scarborough football, it seemed, was turning a corner, the dark days of summer 2007 all of a sudden seemed a long time ago.

By mid May, the rumour mill was in overdrive over who would be competing in the Wearside League for the 2009-10 season. Along with Town, no fewer than 6 other sides were mentioned, for a maximum of three available places. This was firmed up to three full applications, then reduced to two when a Wallsend based side had to withdraw their application after not being able to secure a suitable ground. Town's main worry was the geographical location. Forced to look northwards as no Step 7 league existed in Yorkshire, Town would have to travel as far north as Jarrow and Boldon, almost on the banks of the River Tyne, and would face to Cumbrian sides – Cleator Moor Celtic and Windscale – a 400 mile round trip – something non existent at Step 7 football. Far from the 1920's when the constitution included *'only clubs with 13 miles radius of Sunderland General Post Office will be considered for membership'*, the Wearside League was feeling the full force of many unrepresented Northern areas on the Football Pyramid. North East Counties League football was not going to be possible – the ground would not be able to be improved enough in time, as the recently shown plans had caused a local outcry. Floodlights it seemed, were going to be a much bigger problem then first thought. Despite the locals allowing a whole leisure centre, complete with floodlit Astroturf pitch to be built just over ten years ago, they were not happy with the impact another set would apparently have.

Summer 2009

On June 2, Town were accepted into the Wearside League, a two step jump from (unofficially) Step 9 of the Teesside League Division 2. After a presentation, then a question and answer session, which supplemented an information pack Town had distributed to the league clubs in advance, a vote was taken and Town were admitted alongside Houghton Town, from (unofficially) the step 8 Durham Alliance, in which they had competed as Sunderland South – well within the 13 mile radius of Sunderland's post office. The constitution was set, with 19 clubs and three league 3 cups – the League Cup, The Sunderland Shipowners Charity Cup and the Monkwearmouth Charity Cup plus the North Riding Senior Cup. The club was also interested in the FA Vase, but without floodlights already in place it was impossible to be accepted.

Within ten days of the news, the club announced it had secured shirt and programme sponsors for the upcoming season, and talks were well under way to sell the first advertising boards at the GPCSC base. The kit was to change from the Red and White stripes donated by Sheffield United, to a Red and Black striped home kit, with Dark and Light Blue stripes continuing as the away kit. The excitement and the realism of the forthcoming season was enhanced further with the announcement of the Cup draws – Annfield Plain would visit Pindar in the Shipowners, Town would travel to Willington in the League Cup and would have a home tie against Houghton Town in the Monkwearmouth.

Admission prices were set at £2 for adults, £1 concessions and free for Under 16s ready for the new season, with the introduction of a Season Ticket which would offer entrance to all the home league games for £30. The Travel suits, polo shirts and rain jackets all gained sponsorship also, which was vital as Town were to start the season with 5 consecutive away trips to finance – four of which were 150 mile round trips. With win bonuses to pay to the players as well, the costs involved meant that every penny really counted, as and such the committee worked tirelessly to secure as much financial support as they could through more sponsorship opportunities, such as a 'Big Square Deal' where space could be bought on a board which would be behind where photographs were taken when presenting Man of the Match awards, and a prediction competition also began.

Cook chose to add only two new players to the ranks over summer in preparation for the new adventure. Luke Jenkinson, a 20 year old striker who had finished top scorer in the Scarborough and District League for Edgehill joined along with 23 year old centre back Neil Waterfield. Waterfield joined the club from Teesside Football League Division 1 side Fishburn Park, and had won the League's player of the season in what had been a distinctly average season for the Whitby –based outfit. Both players had previously been members of Scarborough FC's Centre of Excellence up to the Under 16 level, and as such, knew what to expect with a structured training regime. A departure looked on the cards as Nathan Cook spent pre season with League 2 side Grimsby Town, ironically appearing for them in a friendly against Scarborough Athletic, but their loss was Town's gain as they chose not to offer him a deal leaving him free to develop further during the coming season alongside his childhood friends.

JULY 2009

There was no change from last season as the first 5 games would all be away this year. However this was to allow more time for ground improvements at Pindar rather than any cricketing reasons. With this came both advantages – in the fact that by mid-August a quarter of the away trips were out of the way, and disadvantages – mainly starting life in a much higher unknown division without any home comforts. Quietly, Mitch Cook was confident in his sides ability. He wouldn't say exactly what he thought would happen, but that he fancied his team's chances of a good season. Some Town followers knew a little Wearside football – some had watched Kirkbymoorside play, others exiled from Scarborough lived in deepest Wearside, all were confident. It sounded arrogant, and to others it probably was, but they didn't know what Town had, and they weren't supporting a club that had derived from an ex Football League side in very recent memory.

Waterfield and Jenkinson got their first taste of Town action at Tadcaster Albion, another NCEL side. The team had been back in training for a month already. The beach and hills surrounding the Town had been hammered, and the rustiness was further removed in the game which, continuing Town's impressive friendly performances, led to a 3-1 victory. Jenkinson signalled, that despite the step up, he was ready with two goals before half time. This boded well, as two days previously the plotting of the season had begun in earnest with the release of the first months fixtures. Town would begin at Jarrow, 5th placed last time out with just 3 home defeats all season, followed by a local derby at Kirkbymoorside, then Ryhope, Willington and Annfield Plain. Saturday-Wednesday-Saturday-Wednesday-Saturday, before Wednesday then Saturday at home. Guisborough Town HC FC – essentially a reserve side of Northern League side Guisborough Town would provide the opposition for the first home game, then Houghton Town would visit in the cup to complete the first month. 7 games in 21 days – a nice hectic start to the season. The beach and hills would hopefully give an edge.

Round the corner from Pindar; Eastway, the home of Scarborough and District League Champions Eastfield St James played host to Town's next friendly 12 days later, and a bumper crowd of 210 turned out for a game that really was the talk of the community. Town used the warm up well, fielding almost a different side in both halves, with local goalkeeper Paul Robinson playing 90 minutes for Town due to a lack of available goalkeeper. Robinson was ex Scarborough FC himself and, although conceding first, was troubled infrequently. The game was marred by an ankle injury to Joel Ramm, which looked serious enough to rule him out of the start of the season. Josh Greening also wouldn't start the season for Town as he had joined up with Darren Clough and taken the opportunity to try his hand higher up the football pyramid for Pickering Town in the NCEL Premier, scoring 2 goals in his first 3 friendly appearances.

It was a mad dash to Hall Road Rangers for the final pre season fixture, which had a 7pm kick off. Pulling into the car park of the ground and social club, it was obviously that something wasn't right. No minibus from Scarborough in sight. A distinct lack of cars in the car park. The game was off, it transpired, due to rabbit holes on the pitch making it unsafe! One wonders whether they had suddenly appeared an hour before kick off, or had they been there all day? Both sides, it seemed were disappointed with the postponement. Town had wanted another chance to test themselves at a higher level, and another big result would have left them brimming with confidence for the season opener, and Hall Road were looking forward to Town providing 'tougher opposition than their recent opposition' – despite the fact that they had just faced Askern Villa (honestly – their media-savvy chairman changed the name from the less memorable Askern Welfare a year before) of the North East Counties League Division 1! Town's reputation was definitely growing.

AUGUST 2009

So it was the Perth Green Community Centre, the home of Jarrow FC, where Town had their first foray into the Wearside League and the difference was immediate. Town were playing at a ground with the pitch fully enclosed, hard standing surrounding the perimeter and an entrance fee being charged for the privilege of watching. After 20 minutes, the difference on the pitch was obvious. Town had held the lion's share of possession, but after needlessly squandering it 25 yards out from their own goal, Jarrow striker Kris Goss had taken full opportunity and curled the ball past an unexpecting and wrongly-positioned Rob Clark to put the Tynesiders a goal to the good. Not used to falling behind very often, and with lingering doubts over falling behind in their first game at the higher level, it was wondered how the game would now pan out. Jarrow had very little say in what happened next. Robbie Hawkes squared the game almost immediately and on the stroke of half time Luke Jenkinson carried his good pre season form into the season swivelling neatly to put Town 2-1 ahead. The second half began with Town outsmarting a young official. A short corner routine was expertly worked and the ball ended in the Jarrow net. Embarrassed, Jarrow appealed to the assistant referee. He raised his flag, the referee jogged over to ask why, and the goal was disallowed for an illegal corner. Not the first time Town's inventive quick thinking would leave the match officials with tough decisions to make, and certainly not the last. By full time two became six, Jenkinson had bagged himself the match ball, and right back Dean Craig had even found time to venture forward, beat a couple of men and hit the top corner for an early goal-of –the-season contender. Town made the journey back down for the banks of the Tyne sitting on top of the League.

Four days later, Kirkbymoorside were the hosts. The Moorsiders were embarking on their second Wearside season, after making the step up from the Teesside Football League First Division as runners up, and were Town's 'local derby' of the season. A 2-2 opening day draw at Annfield Plain suggested that Town may be in for a sterner test from Kirkby, with Towns unknown quantity tag somewhat diminished. 230 people packed into the Kirkby Mills ground to see Town race into a 3-0 half time lead and effectively kill the game. Jenkinson scored again, looping a header from a Mark Barber long throw over a Kirkby keeper stuck in no man's land, Wayne Brooksby doubled the advantage with a well placed shot from an acute angle, and skipper Georgie Rose burst through on the end of an excellent short passing move to roll the ball calmly past the onrushing keeper. The third away game in succession was to prove a decisive one, with a Nathan Cook double, including an 89th minute 25 yard screamer giving Town an extremely hard fought 2-1 victory away at Ryhope Colliery Welfare – a team who would find themselves entrenched in the title race. Ex Northern League team Willington, a County Durham side with a rich history including FA Amateur Cup finals and Wembley appearances but who had fallen on tough times, were steamrollered 7-1 at their own Hall Road ground, a magnificent example of the traditional Northern non league football ground with ageing stand. A third Nathan Cook penalty in 3 games gave Town all three points at Annfield Plain, banishing the demons of Scarborough FC's 4-1 defeat in the North Eastern League back in the sixties which the Derwent Park sides programme said they were aiming for a repeat of, and left Town in the position of:

P 5 W 5 GF 19 GA 4 PTS 15

a return beyond the expectations of the club as they found their feet at this higher level. This led Town to their first home game in the division on Wednesday August 26 kindly against Guisborough Town HC who had picked up just 4 points from their opening 5 games and had crashed to a 5-2 defeat at Jarrow just 4 days previously. The Pindar ground had seen drastic improvements since spectators last visited in May. The ground was now enclosed by two 6 foot wooden fences, dugouts were in place and in time for the game two sides of the ground had a permanent concrete post and double rail fence in place, with the other two sides roped off for the time being. The record attendance was broken again as 261 people turned up, and tested the grounds other new improvement – a pay booth. Such an entrance was able to make a huge difference – besides the obvious of making the compulsory job of charging an entrance easy, it gave a place to sell the programmes and raffle tickets, and as such made many more people dig into their pockets who previously may not have done so. On the pitch Guisborough were dismantled with a far from vintage 6-0 victory – a scoreline which makes it hard to justify the term 'far from vintage'! Jenkinson scored his second hat trick of the season taking his tally to 7 in 6 games and 17 year old Matty Brown, yet to start a game for Town, entered as a 60th minute substitute and scored a quick fire double.

Brown was handed his first start the following Saturday, as Mitch Cook looked to rotate and rest his squad for the Monkwearmouth Charity Cup 1st Round tie against fellow Wearside newcomers Houghton Town. The game also saw a debut for 18 year old Danny Jenkinson, a tough tackling full back, and first starts of the season for Joe Danby and for Joel Ramm as he returned from his pre season injury. Brown underlined his obvious talent and demonstrated both the strength in depth of the squad, and the ability of the younger players, who would be more than able to play at this level, as Houghton Towns spoiling tactics came undone. After constantly blocking any attempts for quick free kicks, kicking the ball away and persistent fouling, breaking up any momentum Town could gain, Houghton conceded an innocuous free kick just inside their own half and for the first time, retreated from the ball, Brown took the opportunity to strike the ball over the keeper, still stood on the edge of his penalty box, into the unguarded net. Joel Ramm celebrated his comeback with a second goal 5 minutes later and Town cruised into the Second Round. As Town were to find out throughout the season, their style of football, and expectations they held, both on and off the pitch were not always even remotely similar to their opponents. And this could cause serious friction. Houghton left Town with a moan – the pitch wasn't good enough, the facilities weren't good enough, the hospitality wasn't good enough, nor the referee. But as with pretty much every team, including Town, moaning only seems to happen and be significant when you've lost the game.

September 2009

Mitch Cook fervently believed that his team didn't always learn enough in their high scoring crushing victories, and as such, the odd defeat was useful for the team in their development. The first defeat of the season came at ex-Northern League side Easington Colliery on a rain swept night on the Durham coast. Again, arrival at the ground showed the progress that had been made. Boasting covered seating and floodlights, with hard standing surrounding the pitch, Easington was a ground to make most of the Wearside League jealous and it signified another little step in the right direction for Town that they were competing at better facilities. The game itself, albeit slightly ruined by the cold wind blowing in from the North Sea just some 300 metres away, saw two teams who tried to play football on the floor, with Easington showing a little more maturity. For the first serious time, Towns tactics seemed to be found out. Easington pressed high, meaning Towns short pass and move football became deeper and deeper and the system of playing short from the goalkeeper became tougher. Town picked up another two yellow cards as they struggled to break down the Collieries resolute defence, and along with Ryhope CW, Town had found themselves an opponent who could keep the pace. Some neutrals who had come to watch posted on the ever-so-popular internet message boards proclaiming the game to be of a much higher standard than they had come to expect from the Wearside League, whilst other neutrals who had come to watch – spotted in the Houghton Town dugout at Pindar just three days earlier, took much pleasure in Easington's goal - the only one of the game. There was more success for the under 16's midweek however as they romped to 5-3 away win at Grimsby Town once more showcasing the talent that Town would be able to call upon in the coming years.

After the midweek defeat, the visit of Coxhoe Athletic couldn't have come at a better time. Town had dropped to second on goal difference, as Ryhope joined them on 18 points from 7 games.

Ashbrooke Belford House had amassed 15 points from 6, and Teesside Athletic had 11 from 5, meaning that Town needed a win – if one bad result in 7 meant that the table remained so tight, then Town couldn't afford to drop many more points early in the season. Coxhoe on the other hand had had an awful start. 6 defeats from 6 games, a goal difference of minus 19 and only one goal scored away from home. So, of course with 83 minutes gone the score stood at Scarborough Town 0-1 Coxhoe Athletic, and the honeymoon period of Wearside football had well and truly disappeared. The next 7 minutes proved a point. Luke Jenkinson drilled home his eighth goal of the season, low and hard from the edge of the box and Robbie Hawkes, if he wasn't already, began to become a crowd favourite. With 5 minutes to go he beat his man and hit the net. With the sighs of relief still audible around Pindar, he picked up the ball and replicated it. With Coxhoe broken Joe Danby saw his chance and picked out the top corner from all of 30 yards. 4-1, Town had shown in just 7 minutes what they were capable of.

The tricky spell continued the following week when Annfield Plain visited Pindar in the Preliminary Round of the Shipowners cup as at half time Town found themselves 2-0 down. Scarborough had been hit by an Indian summer, well as Indian summer like as Scarborough can be, swelling the crowd to just shy of 150. By now the ground had improved further, the pitch was now fully railed down all four sides and subtle improvements began to be made to the matchday experience. The tirelessly working behind the scenes team were able to run a more efficient operation, ranging from picking up tips from away visits, acting upon feedback from visitors and adding any ideas to make everything around Scarborough Town as professional-esque as possible. Striving for professionalism was not to come at expense though – nothing was extravagant, and everything was done with cost in mind. The matchday programme was something that Town were rightly proud of, well sponsored, but not at the expense of dominating the content, and packed with personally written, thoughtful articles rather than internet copies. It would not have been out of place many leagues higher, yet only cost £1, as anything more than this would begin to make people think about buying one rather than just using one of their pound coins change they had just got after paying their admittance. The profit of the programme was driven up further by the dedication Town's volunteers went to in order minimise costs for the club. By receiving the programmes from the printers unfolded and unstapled, it saved 3 pence. So that was the programme editor and a couple of the committee members Friday nights sorted! Over the season, and with around 100 programmes printed per game, it saved the club a few more pounds and highlighted just how committed and financially conscious those following the club were. On the pitch, the players were conscious that they could still progress through this tie and came out all guns blazing after some stern half time words. Joel Ramm pulled the first back, before lady luck smiled, as Rob Clark brought down an onrushing striker. The card was only yellow – if that didn't incense Plain the fact he then saved the penalty did. Luke Jenkinson then found a half yard of space on the edge of the box and drove low and hard into the bottom corner to level things up. Town huffed and puffed but couldn't grab a winner and so, for the first time, Pindar saw extra time. After 90 minutes in the stifling heat, the game fizzled out – and so to penalties it went.

The referee didn't seek police advice for the shootout – the end nearest the changing rooms and the spectator exit was chosen. Plain opened the scoring, then Luke Jenkinson walked up first for Town and walked back having blazed the ball over the top of the goal. Joe Danby hit the net then Clark saved to level the scores, a penalty apiece was converted but then Hawkes penalty crashed down off the bar without crossing the line leaving Plain 3-2 up, with the chance to seal a place in Round 1, and with it a long trip to Cumbria to face Cleator Moor Celtic. Whether this was on Will Jarvis-Smith's mind as he stepped up remains to be known, but despite sending Clark the wrong way, the penalty only hit the post. Joel Ramm banished any memories of Teesside Athletic Reserves back in April and the game went to sudden death. Rob Clark proved that lady luck was well and truly on his side as he saved his third penalty of the afternoon and Carl Cook fired home to give Town victory to the relief of almost everyone within the ground.

As the club was now becoming accustomed to the Wearside League, it was clear that there were many changes from the previous season. For a start, Town had accumulated 15 bookings by mid September – when last season had seen four in the full season – two of which were shown in Darren Clough's two yellow card dismissal, and one for Mark Barber which the referee gave to 'calm the game down' as the opponents were moaning at him at the amount of yellow cards they had received! Matchday operations were running much more smoothly with the players receiving hot food after matches through a deal struck with the on-site burger van. One thing didn't change though as the under 19s started their new campaign midweek against Pontefract Collieries, after starting last years season there in emphatic style, the same happened with Town running out 10-2 victors. As with Darren Clough last season, despite Josh Greening now playing his senior football in the NCEL for Pickering Town, his under 19 registration remained in Scarborough, and to stop himself being forgotten he hit 4 goals with returning debutant Sean Exley, who had rejoined the under 19s after leaving a couple of years previously, scoring a hat trick.

Boldon CA came to Town the following Saturday fresh from a 4-1 victory over Easington Colliery. Another extremely healthy crowd of 155 visited Pindar and the majority were settled as Mark Barber gave Town the lead after an even opening 20 minutes. Shortly before the break the game was halted for 15 minutes as Boldon's Dean Mckeown smashed into his own post whilst clearing the ball which required a trip to Scarborough hospital for what would be diagnosed as knee ligament damage. This somewhat deflated the visitors and Town turned the screw after the break with a brace from Robbie Hawkes and Luke Jenkinson's 9th goal in eleven games giving a 4-0 victory and, just as importantly, a clean sheet.

Bedlington Terriers were the visitors to Pickering for Town's first foray into the FA Youth Cup under the current set up. It was an unknown experience. For the last few years the under 19 alliance had been fairly static. As such, you had a pretty good idea in every game what you were about to face – shocks were pretty much few and far between. The youth cup offered a real adventure for those watching and a real chance to make a name for yourself if you were on the pitch. As the flagship competition for youth football a run meant more and more scouts watching games – not that the under 19s weren't on the radar already, and a chance to see how good the youth of Scarborough actually were. Of course one subtle difference in this competition was that the Youth Cup was under 18, not under 19 – but this mattered little to Town. 3-1 victors 90 minutes later, the Under 18s were through, to face another northern club in either Prudhoe or Ryton – the latter knocking Scarborough FC out of the 2004-5 competition.

Hartlepool were next to visit Pindar, with the omens not brilliant. 100 years ago, West Hartlepool Expansion had brushed aside Scarborough FC 3-0 in an FA Cup Preliminary Round tie, and the last time sides from Scarborough and Hartlepool had met in mid April 1999 Peter Beardsley had inspired the Pools to a 3-0 victory in front of over 5000, which ultimately led to Hartlepool finishing the season just 3 points ahead of the relegated Boro. The 180 who were watching this one though probably expected a different result. With the Pools on a run of 5 straight defeats, it was no surprise when Robbie Hawkes opened the scoring. A red card a-piece changed the game, as firstly, with half time approaching Luke Jenkinson saw a straight red for kicking out off the ball, and then just after half time the same offence saw Hartlepool down to ten. The difference? Hartlepool's happened to be their goalkeeper. No substitute on the bench, Nathan Cook easily dispatched the penalty and then Robbie Hawkes took centre stage, hitting the net another three times, his second four goal blitz in a Town shirt. So, the month ended with Town on top, 27 points from ten games, with 38 goals scored already – a good response to the Easington game – the lads were learning – another step on the road of development, and playing the entertaining football they were was a nice by product.

The start of the adventure. Captain Georgie Rose does the pre match formalities at the start of Town's first ever home game v Grangetown YCC.

Matt Perry (hidden) hooks home Town's first home goal at the McCains Sports Field n the same game.

The town word spreads. Robbie Hawkes sees the space whilst over 250 people watch him in Town's first home game in the Wearside League v Guilsborough Town FC.

The stormy sky matched the mood of the hosts as Town travelled to Grangetown (one of the better grounds in the league!) and came away with a 7-0 victory.

hts out. Town's valiant
odlit attempt is thwarted.

Dean Craig's ever dependable left foot looks to create another scoring chance.

Luke Jenkinson goes for goal. His first season with the club would return 21 goals in just 28 appearances.

With time running out, Robbie Hawkes goes for goal v Easington Colliery....

....and scores!

Josh Greening pokes home the winner v Ryhope CW to secure the Wearside League Title at the first time of asking....

....and Rob Clark runs the length of the pitch to get in on the celebrations.

INSET Georgie Rose lifts the 112 year old Sunderland Shipowners Cup.

SCARBOROUGH TOWN FC - TeesideLeague Second Division Champions 2008/2009

SCARBOROUGH
TOWN F.C.
The Commun Based Football Club

Not forgetting the U19s - Northern Alliance League and Cup double winners 2008/2009

October 2009

Windy Wolviston was a forgettable afternoon for anyone who had picked their home game against Town. Wolviston itself was an extremely pleasant place as was the football club, however, as they were recovering from pitch trouble, playing football there was extremely hard. Much work and money had been injected into the ground, and it was unfortunate that it couldn't have any more time to bed before being played upon, as it just wasn't ready. The game itself passed quickly. Robbie Hawkes found the top corner after 20 minutes, then Town survived the second half as Wolviston beat Clark with a tapped-in finish after hitting the crossbar, but the Referees assistant's flag, blowing viciously in the wind, meant that Town left with all 3 points. As the only club in the Wearside with a programme containing a buy-one-get-one-free offer for a Big Mac at major sponsors McDonalds, perhaps the afternoon wasn't entirely forgettable.

Two long trips in five days beckoned, as firstly the under 18s continued the FA Youth Cup run at Prudhoe Town, and left with a comfortable 4-0 victory, which put the team just one round away from the League sides, then Town headed on the first of their Cumbrian trips, with Cleator Moor Celtic providing the next hurdle to overcome, in the Sunderland Shipowners Cup 1st Round. Celtic were firmly mid table, but had a home record consisting of 5 wins out of 5. Something had to give, and, by now, you get how many of these things worked, Town ended that run – in some style. With ex-Celtic, and now England goalkeeper Scott Carson watching his younger brother between the sticks, Town had a 3-0 half time lead, which by the close had ended 8-2 – the most Town would ever score in an away game, in their second longest ever trip (Windscale being a further 6 miles). The trip didn't seem so far on the way back.

Silksworth's newly appointed manager Chris Lindstedt made a bold claim in his programme notes for the midweek meeting when he stated – *'I watched them in August...and left convinced I had witnessed this seasons league champs. I believe that any team that finishes above them will undoubtedly be champions'* and saw Town open up a five point lead after a far from spectacular 2-0 win with a goal in each half. Away evening trips were tough, with 7.30 kick off meaning it wasn't always easy for the players to reach the ground on time – but this was nothing compared to what was to come six months later. It was a game that Town won without ever really gaining a rhythm, and one which could have been put to bed at half time had that happened – as New Marske found out the next Saturday. Again, New Marske came with a reputation – runners up last season, winners the season before. A couple too many draws saw New Marske sitting in sixth place when they visited Pindar, for what would be the first of at least 3 matches between the two– more if both teams progressed in the cups also. This one was the North Riding Senior Cup – the competition which had seen Town knocked out at their first attempt last year. With Luke Jenkinson suspended, Joel Ramm was thrown up front, and repaid the faith showed in him, in double quick time – a flick header, a close range volley then a measured 25 yard chip completing an astonishing hat trick, with just 17 minutes on the clock. After this restart, Town won a corner, Patterson dummied and Rose made it 4, and with less than 25 minutes on the clock, Brooksby was needlessly fouled when he had his back to goal just inside the area, and Hawkes sent the keeper the wrong way to make it 5-0. New Marske showed some resilience where others would have folded with a goal either side of half time, but after the wake-up call this gave, Joe Danby and Dean Craig added to the scoresheet to give Town a trip to Whitby based Fishburn Park – who Town had essentially leapfrogged from being the division below last season to the division above.

With perimeter barriers now completed along the bottom goal and the dugout side of the pitch, finally, no more rope was needed to separate the supporters from the pitch and the next phase on improvement was complete. Little by little it was looking even more like a football ground rather than a school field. The problem was could it improve further at a rate to keep up with the team? Floodlights and hard standing were still being fought for, but no headway had been made as yet. It seemed that wasn't the only problem Town had – New Marske's manager, dismissed during the game, believed that Town should not be a Wearside League side as they were an Academy side. Obviously, if he had beaten the 'Academy Side' I'm sure he wouldn't have minded them being in the league? So if Town shouldn't be in an adult league on the football pyramid due to their youthful nature, where should they be? The under 19 alliance wasn't really aiding the older players progression as much anymore. The team had several over 19 year olds and, as midweek would show, the youngest players still had a long way to go. On the flip side, Town were receiving acclaim for other areas of the football community – groundhoppers who had seen Town and left impressed passed their comments on, and notably, so had match officials – two of whom were kind enough to share their opinions, in return for remaining anonymous:-

"I had heard off other referee's and from reading the non league websites that Scarborough had been playing some cracking football and were a breath of fresh air to the league - they didn't fail to disappoint. The opposition were frustrated and proceeded to kick 'hells bells' out of Scarborough who were three or four goals up. Fair play to Town, they never shied out of a tackle and remained professional where a lot of younger players would have got involved and let their heads go. The match finished with Scarborough easily beating the opposition who had six men booked and received a fine from the County F.A.

People often think that referee's are robots and don't have a hobby! Most however used to play the game they love and appreciate a good game of football, Scarborough were both aesthetically pleasing to watch and referee and Mitch Cook instilled discipline into the team which made referee's lives a lot easier. They were a club referee's used to look forward to going to and despite the journey most referees would have went their each week if they could.

From talking to other clubs and referees I know that Scarborough did upset a few teams in the league possibly due to their quality which may have been perceived as arrogance. In my opinion the club was well run and had the backing of a good chairman, followed by secretary, through the coach Mitch Cook and then onto the team. They had a solid backbone through the club and were lucky enough to attract a large crowd of spectators to both home and away fixtures." Whilst another produced a more concise, yet as valid, opinion on Scarborough Town, commenting that Town were *"by far the most professional club in the league, with the biggest support and were fouled the most but reacted the least"* A testament to the football education they had gained.

The FA Youth Cup adventure came to an end midweek with a trip to Bootham Crescent to take on the Under 18s of local rivals York City. Well, York City had been Scarborough FC's main rivals, though the Under 19s teams had not faced each other for some time, and Scarborough Town were not on the radar of York City supporters rivalries. Facing a team containing full time YTS professionals in front of almost 400 spectators was going to be tough for Town's youngsters, so luck is always appreciated. Especially when it comes in the form of captain Joe Danby blocking a York defender's pass to the extent that it flew over the head of the stranded City keeper. An almost identical goal was scored by Cesc Fabregas for Arsenal at Sunderland in October 2010, but he was simply copying what happened at Bootham Crescent just under a year earlier. The occasion did get to Town though; York ran out hugely comfortable 3-1 winners and progressed to the first round proper. The tie gave a benchmark – there was a chance that some of the opposition could go on to forge full time long careers in the game – that was what all the Scarborough lads aspired to.

The month closed with the news that Windscale were to resign from the league. Not again – another league table to be changed, this time it was Ryhope who would suffer most after winning 5-1 against the Cumbrians back in August. For Town it meant the saving of the costs associated with travelling over to Cumbria, but the mixed effect of losing a home match, with the attendance and other income that brought. Every game held expense though. The players were paid a modest sum – in the form of a win bonus only – but of course, they seemed to win quite a lot. So, no result on the pitch meant they didn't

get rewarded off it. If money was a motivating factor for any of them they both hid it well, and were doing rather well out of it.
Josh Greening returned to the club to boost the striking options ahead of the return 'local derby' with Kirkbymoorside. A filthy day prevented a 200 plus crowd and highlighted that anything to protect spectators from the elements and mud could lead to an attendance boom – if only it was that simple. Derby days had always been special in the town, with various different clubs being the derby attraction depending on what division Boro were playing in at the time. Ten seasons previous, it had been Hull City, with the two derby games attracting a combined attendance of 16711. In more recent times the stand out derby's were York City – 4586 had packed the McCain Stadium on Boxing Day 2004 to see York destroyed 5-1, then just over a year later, another 4057 saw Chris Hughes' late late leveller to give Boro a point against a York side that would end the season 26 points ahead. It was that typical derby that was at Pindar – league positions were irrelevant and just as Town routinely did to others, reputations were almost laughed at. Kirkbymoorside scored 5. Town slumped to their first ever home league defeat in their history in some style. Not getting to grips with the weather, Town fell behind from distance, but it seemed normal service would be resumed when Joel Ramm touched home the equalizer. Less than a minute later, as Town usually routinely did after conceding, the Moorsiders were 2-1 up, and by half time it was three. Three became five midway through the second half, and it took two late Town strikes to give the scoreline slightly more respectability from a Town point of view.
7-2, 3-5, 7-2 is perhaps the most unlikely three game result combination you will ever see, but is exactly what Town produced as Silksworth came to Pindar the following week, and it had mirrors of the last 7-2 after a devastating first half took the game out of the reach of the visitors. 4-0 at half time, Joe Danby tapped home a fifth before two identical goals brought Silksworth ever so slightly back into the game – identical as each other, but also identical to one which New Marske had scored in that game with the identical scoreline. Deep diagonal balls to the back post seemed to be the way to beat Town. Just teams didn't get the chance to use it very

often – and the times when they did were usually because Town had already taken their foot off the gas. The game saw another hat trick for Luke Jenkinson – his third and Town's seventh of the season.
By the close of the month, there had been a u-turn – Windscale were back! The trip to Cumbria was back, and thankfully the league was continuing unaffected. A second club to do so, after Silksworth had beaten its problems and survived a month earlier.

November 2009

North Riding Senior Cup duty came next, with an away trip to Fishburn Park, who last season were a division above Town, but now were a division below. Away from home, back to the more-primitive facilities of the Teesside League, cold, windy – could any more factors point towards Town being giant-killed? Fishburn would be Town's closest away trip of the season, a mere 18 miles away, and once more, an indicator of how much football had changed. Town fans had been used to a rivalry with Whitby in the Scarborough FC days. Well, partly a rivalry, as the teams never really met, as the one division gap in 2006 was the closest the teams had ever been. Most meetings had tended to come in the North Riding Senior Cup, but Boro rarely put out their best eleven. 2001 had seen Whitby embarrass Boro in the FA Cup of all competitions. 1800 had attended the 4th qualifying round clash, and seen Whitby outplay a Scarborough side who didn't seem to know what had hit them and win 3-1. Now, Town had their first local derby of sorts, but not even against Whitby's senior side. Situated at the top of quite a rise, Broomfield Park is exposed, with no cover, and barely enough space around the pitch surrounds and the perimeter fence to walk. For a long time there had been talk that this game would be switched to Whitby Town's Turnbull Ground, but it transpired that Fishburn didn't want that – they, of course, wanted the advantage and a bigger, better pitch would just play into Town's hands. Home advantage was the leveller. Town started brightly, Josh Greening rounding the keeper early on to put Town ahead. But the possession didn't materialise into anything more, the referee wasn't going to let the higher ranked away side moan at every physical tackle and get rewarded. A speculative effort flashed past debutant keeper Ricky Ossai, half time was 1-1. Robbie Hawkes was thrown on, abuse was thrown by the Whitby-folk, and chaos ensued as Hawkes made his mark 20 minutes after the restart. Felled for a penalty, the home side weren't happy, the supporters had seen it all before apparently.

It was because they were playing Scarborough and they always get preferential treatment. Having never played Town before, nor Fishburn Park having played Scarborough FC, one wonders logically how this decision was arrived at. But it was to get worse. Town thought it wasn't their day and Fishburn began to believe that this horrible Scarborough bias was to come to nothing as the penalty was saved. But no, wait, the assistant flagged. The keeper was close to the six yard line when he saved it. Typical, Scarborough bias again. So it was to be a retake. Hawkes stepped up again, went a different way, but the same result – saved again, but not the rebound. Smashed home from close range and Town were back in front. The referee now had another problem on his hands. The Fishburn manager wouldn't stop smoking in his dugout a problem compounded by the fact that the manager would not even acknowledge the assistant as he had awarded the retake. It was close to five minutes later that play restarted, and ten minutes later the first disgruntled home fans began to slope off, murmuring and chuntering as they left. Greening wrapped the game up ten minutes from time and Town had reached the third round where the 'big boys' would enter.

Cup duty continued for another fortnight, as firstly Town went to Willington, the sight of their biggest away victory to date in the League Cup preliminary round. A night of freezing fog, floodlights that didn't quite light up all the pitch and another irate home manager saw Town sneak home 2-1. Dominant in possession as usual, Town had conceded sloppily and then made the game harder than it needed to be. The 52 strong crowd saw a special goal to win the game however, as Greening bagged his 5th in 3 games since rejoining the club with an exquisite chip from 25 yards. This meant a first round tie at home to Teesside Athletic, who were 7 points behind Town, in third place in the League, but with two games in hand and were the divisions most miserly defence with only 11 goals conceded in 12 games and a solitary defeat to Town's next opponents – Ryhope CW.

And so to 'ballgate' a series of events which thankfully overshadowed a horrendous afternoon. The third different cup in three weeks saw Town and Ryhope CW face each other in the Monkwearmouth Charity Cup. On the pitch Town started brightly with the fluent pass and move football not allowing Ryhope to get a foot in the game. As half time approached at 2-0 it seemed Town were being rewarded for their play. 20 minutes later and it was 2-2, as high balls into Town's were box were not dealt with. As the game entered the last twenty minutes, Town were down to ten men. Three subs had already been used and Robbie Hawkes had received a horror tackle that would put him out for four months. Nathan Cook scored the penalty, but the card had only been yellow. With injury time looming, Town's ten couldn't hang on, and the equaliser came. Extra time was denied even crueller, as Ramm shielded the ball out for a goal kick, which to his horror was awarded as a corner. He then chested down the resulting inswinger, which to his horror was seen by the referee as handball, and to all of the Town followers horror, the penalty was smashed home. There was barely time for kick off. Town's Monkwearmouth Cup challenge was over – with a demoralising defeat against the title rivals, and a serious injury to a key player.
What had happened on the pitch was only half of the afternoon though. Half time had seen beer poured from the bar windows onto people below. With such disregard for their pints, the recession obviously hadn't hit these people, who coincidentally hadn't been seen at the ground before, so perhaps they weren't local to Scarborough or regularly watched Town -perhaps they had only seen them play once before, back in August? By full time the supporters of each club disliked each other even more, fuelled by what they had witnessed on the field, tensions ran high off the pitch. Not content with cruelly having the last laugh on the pitch, they thought they had had it off the pitch also. Playing at a leisure centre attached to a school however means one important acronym – CCTV. The bag of balls and training equipment that had gone missing and then appeared in the Sunderland suburbs was an accident. The chap who the CCTV showed looking around, checking who else was in his proximity before grabbing the bags and running to the car park had

thought that it was the away teams equipment obviously. Well at least the misunderstanding was cleared up through a series of phonecalls between the two clubs, and the gear was returned. Well, returned meaning if Town wanted it back they would have to drive up to Ryhope and get it themselves.

The balls were back as the league programme resumed the following week with the visit of Willington. There was no such scare as the League Cup fixture two weeks before as the bigger, flatter pitch allowed Town to race into a 3-0 lead at half time, that became 8-1 by the conclusion of the game, with Nathan Cook continuing Towns indifference from the penalty spot, scoring one then having one saved as Town were awarded two spot kicks in the last third of the game. Town had put 15 past Willington in two league games. This was tough on Willington's keeper Chris Sawyer however who easily stopped 15 being 25, and had the admiration of Town's followers. The same can not quite be said for dugout-based Paul Mullen. After voicing his displeasure at his team mates for 65 minutes, he promptly brought himself on, despite the fact it looked like his better playing days were over. Trying to shield the ball on the edge of his own box for Sawyer to come out and claim whilst holding off a Town player, desperate to add their name to the scoresheet for the fifth goal, he poked the ball past his own keeper for an own goal. He then picked up a yellow card, before finally crudely conceding a penalty, in which one of his team mates saw red for overprotesting at. The three points were massively welcome, as Ryhope defeated Kirkbymoorside to keep their four point advantage, with Town still having one game in hand. Town had ended the game with 8 teenagers on the pitch, five of them being just 17 years old.

The intriguingly named Ashbrooke Belford House visited Pindar the week after. Known as being both one of the 'better' sides in the league and perhaps a touch physical. As such, this gave the match more potential of becoming memorable, and it didn't disappoint. The crowd broke the three-figure mark again, despite more poor weather which was becoming a stumbling block. With any improvements being some months away due to the difficulties that were being encountered, a lack of cover and the mud was putting people off. Unlike those who couldn't quite make their mind up in the past on a horrible day, they couldn't be swayed by the 3,500 covered seats that the McCain Stadium had had. Coupled with that it was now impossible to watch Town without getting muddy and unless you were under the Town spell, which left you needing to see the infective brand of football as much as possible, you probably would choose Soccer Saturday and listen to Jeff and Co creating an afternoon of addictive TV that in theory shouldn't be. Watching a TV of someone describing what is happening on another TV shouldn't work! Sometimes even they struggle to do a goal justice, and having already described so many goals as memorable or unbelievable, this is one of those moments. It came from Rob Clark, his second game back in goal. Claiming a cross, he bowled to Nathan Cook, not much further than the edge of his own penalty box. He fed Wayne Brooksby who carried the ball 50 yards, dodging the lunges of the tracking back midfielders. The defenders back tracked, as he fed Josh Greening on the left, who took a touch, looked up and delivered. Arriving was Nathan Cook, who was not letting the ball beat him, taking off he threw himself towards the ball, meeting it with the firmest of diving headers. The Belford House keeper didn't react, Town were ahead and the whole move had taken no more than 15 seconds. By the second half the lead had been doubled by Brooksby when it happened. It had to happen, Ashbrooke's physicality led to a bad tackle, the bad tackle led to a coming together of a dozen players, a punch was thrown and the referee had a battle to restore order. His back was turned to the punch as he had attempted to stop the pushing and shoving elsewhere, but the assistant had seen. After consultation, Town's Matt Perry saw yellow, and Belford House's Lee Harrison saw red. Cook hit his second with ten minutes to play with the aid of a huge deflection, but claimed it sufficiently to be able to complete his hat trick as he found the 'postage stamp' top corner to the goal from 18 yards eight minutes later to give Town an emphatic 4-0 victory. Just as important though, was the clean sheet, the first in eight games.

December 2009

The first news to come out of the club in December was significant...for programme collectors. When Town were to visit Windscale on the first Saturday of the month, Windscale were to issue. It would be their first programme since 1996. The game itself was exciting as well, though Town probably wished it had ended at half time. 3-0 up after 30 minutes, Town were cruising. Cruising so much that defensive midfielder Jamie Patterson had scored his first of the season to become the 13th different Town player to score. By full time it was 3-3 Dean Rogers slamming home an 88th minute equaliser. Town had been cruising far too much. The game in hand had only brought one point – so Ryhope lead by three.
It is unconfirmed that the crowd dipped 3 people below 100 the following Saturday as a protest to Town squandering that 3 goal cushion the week before. But perhaps a downpour, coupled with it being close to Christmas and also bitterly cold at Pindar (which, through no fault of those trying, was still without any improvements) may have also had an impact. The 97 that did attend saw Town continue on the League Cup trail against Teesside Athletic, meaning that Town had now encountered every team in the League. Joel Ramm, who famously (in Scarborough Town terms) hit his 12 minute hat trick earlier in the season against Teesside's near neighbours New Marske, hit two goals in the last three minutes of the first half to send Town in two goals clear. James Kesterton, with a fairly impressive goalscoring record himself (26 goals the previous season, matched already this) pulled one back for Redcar-based Athletic, but Town hung on, showing a side of their game that wasn't frequently seen for an impressive victory. The game saw Billy Logan, who had two goals in two under 19 appearances, make his first team debut for Town in which he was rewarded handsomely with a £7 fine for picking up a yellow card.
The year ended with the postponement of the Sunderland Shipowners Cup quarter Final tie between Town and Jarrow at Pindar,

and began one of the most bizarre set of events, and highlighted one of the most bizarre set of rules in a sequence that would run until March. It was also a time when Scarborough Council announced that football would definitely never be played at the Athletic Ground again, and Pindar was still waiting for a long overdue announcement from the council and Sport England with regards to the planning application.

January 2010

January came, the weather hadn't improved significantly, and so it was three postponements to begin the month. This then meant that with over a month of no football, the Pindar pitch had been somewhat protected. A 9am pitch inspection by a football league official deemed the pitch playable and so Jarrow made the trip to play the quarter final tie. Between 9am and the 1.30pm kick off however, it rained and it poured. The match referee didn't fancy it, despite both teams wanting to get the game played. Match off. Jarrow had travelled 2 hours to be sent home without kicking a ball, and the game was to be played the following Saturday. Jarrow appealed that the game should be switched to their ground, as precedent dictated this. East Durham United folded at the end of the 2008-9 season, but played an important part in what was to come. In their final season, after two postponements of their cup due to their unfit pitch whilst their opponents ground was playable, the league ruled that the tie should be switched. Of course, during the time that this had occurred only one Wearside fixture had been able to take place in the time and no other club had had their cup fixture scheduled twice in the period!

The appeal meant Jarrow were still to come down to Pindar for the second time in 8 days, but that the game was to be played as a league clash whilst the clubs waited for the wisdom of the league management committee. So, league game it was, none of what was happening really bothered the players they just played football. Despite the weather enforced break Town scored five without reply, with doubles for both Nathan Cook and Joe Danby. Ryhope did the same to Houghton Town to remain clear and Cleator Moor Celtic consolidated third spot with a 1-0 win at Kirkbymoorside. The delight over another good victory was soured a few days later, when the news came that Jarrow had won their appeal. Despite only one Wearside game taking place between December 12 and January 16 the tie was to be switched to Jarrow as Town's pitch had been unplayable twice. Again no other tie had even been scheduled twice in this period! It was also the day that it was announced that the revised planning application had gone to Scarborough Borough Council for hard standing and floodlights. As it had been for while, all the funding was in place – all that was needed was the go ahead. As soon as this was given, more changes that didn't require planning permission would also go ahead, including more fencing and a redesign of the changing rooms, including a larger, more spacious officials changing area.

The Under 19s resumed after over two months off with a trip to Garforth Town, which they predictably returned with three points from. 8-0 was the final scoreline, with Billy Logan grabbing a hat-trick. The under 19s found themselves in the most awkward of positions. Stretching back to last season, this was the 14th win in a row. The team hadn't been beaten since Whitby Town had won 2-0 back in March 2008. So this begged the question, what should the under 19s do? The York game had shown the gulf between the professional clubs, with full time youth players, and Town. But the results showed that the Under 19 league was probably not offering that much development to the players anymore.

The players still needed some development. It was the North Riding Senior Cup up next – with Northallerton Town of the Northern League second division providing the opposition. As this was the division which Town wanted to be competing in next season, it would be a good benchmark of what Town could expect week in week out. Of course, one of Town's greatest strengths was their home form and the way they used the Pindar pitch, the way the majority of the crowd created an atmosphere which was mostly alien to the level of football. But unlike Fishburn Park were able to do in the last round, Town lost the advantage, as the game had to be played midweek and the floodlights were still being wrangled over. Therefore 'home' was Whitby Town – linked with GPCSC, through sponsorship coming about with 5 Whitby players working at the college, and with massive links to Mitch Cook, who was part of the 1997 all conquering Whitby Town side that captured the Northern League title, promotion to the Northern Premier (Unibond) League, and the FA Vase at Wembley

Stadium. The match was to have a subdued footnote regardless, as it was to be Wayne Brooksby's last appearance before he headed to Australia, travelling - doing whatever 19 year old's who go travelling do. The match never got going from a Town point of view. An even first half didn't lead to more of the same in the second as Mark Barber, who quietly pulled the strings all season with a range of short and long passing that could destroy teams, pulled up injured. Within a minute Town had lost possession and were a goal behind. Town huffed and puffed on a heavy pitch, but were dealt a cruel blow with 20 minutes left, as Rob Clark could only parry a fierce effort which rebounded off the unlucky Carl Cook and trickled over the line. To run insult into injury, as Town pressed, the gaps at the back grew, Northallerton exploited and ran out 3-0 winners to inflict Town's first ever, and only, three goal defeat. The winners would face Scarborough Athletic, and rightly it was Northallerton Town - saving possibly an embarrassing situation of Scarborough v Scarborough, played anywhere but Scarborough with a further decaying 'stadium' still lying unused and no closer to development.

February 2010

Boldon visited Pindar for the second time for the League Cup Quarter Final in what turned out to be a very one sided affair as Town bounced back from their North Riding Senior Cup disappointment. Ricky Ossai got a run out in goal, as Rob Clark was injured, and was beaten from outside the box after half an hour as Boldon reduced the arrears to 2-1 and at this point the game was on. But as many teams had already found out, and many to come would find out, it took a 90 minute performance to test Town. Boldon switched off for 3 minutes before half time, the score moved from 2-1 to 5-1 and the game was over. The second half saw Town able to conserve energy, playing at a training pace, adding 3 more goals to end with a crushing 8-1 victory and put themselves into the semi final.
Three days later and it was Under 19 duty for five of the team that faced Boldon as they headed down to Glasshoughton. Six different scorers, all of whom had appeared for the first team, fired the Under 19s to their second successive 8-0 away victory. So, up to Jarrow for the third attempt of the Sunderland Shipowners Cup Quarter Final. Ironically, the Pindar pitch was through the winter worst, was completely fit and had held up to the Boldon game well. So typically, Jarrow's wasn't and the game was off, to be replayed in a fortnight. Not many Wearside League clubs regularly issued programmes – many just for Town's visit. Most of those which did were a one or two man effort. When Windscale made the trip over from Cumbria Town could boast a Swedish based contributor for their latest issue, supplementing the usual 4 or 5 regular contributors, and showed once more that the interest in the club spread far and wide. The Cumbrians had had a good month so far – holding Ryhope 1-1 and defeating Easington 2-0. It took 40 minutes for Town to break the deadlock, as Joel Ramm nipped onto a through-ball, in a game which saw both goalkeepers and defences worked hard. Town's was worked even harder when Nathan Cook saw Town's second straight red of the season as he threw himself into a challenge in what was

deemed an unsafe manner. Working hard, Town dug deep and were rewarded for their resolute defending as Josh Greening sprinted clear on what was a rare attack, rounded the keeper and rolled the ball home. Windscale kept pressing, but fizzled out after a late red card of their own, mirroring the reverse fixture, but this time Town held on for a good three points.

And it was off again. Jarrow's pitch still wasn't playable – they hadn't been able to host a home game since November 28. Except they would have on both December 19 and January 9, as the rules state that the game can be switched if the home teams ground is unfit, whilst the oppositions' is playable on two occasions. Now, after two postponements when the ground was unfit at Jarrow but fine at Scarborough the game would be switched back. But no, it wouldn't. The rules didn't apply this time and Town would have to travel to Jarrow in March and, perhaps more importantly, with so many League games left to play, and Town still in two cup competitions also, Town had lost two Saturdays of football in the last three.

March 2010

Two home games, two Cumbrian sets of visitors, as Cleator Moor Celtic were next to fortress Pindar. Boosted by the return of Wayne Brooksby, Town tore into Celtic from the beginning, with Brooksby eager to please – which he did in style with a first half hat trick to give Town a 3-1 interval lead. Such was Town's early confidence that when Celtic had equalised, Town were back in front within a minute, seemingly not even noticing that they had only been drawing briefly. Adding two more in the second half, Town signified that they were building momentum and were ready when (or if) Ryhope slipped up – their lead was 7 points, and Town had 2 games in hand. Conveniently, it happened in midweek, as they could only manage a draw at home to Jarrow – a good result for the side Town were facing the coming Saturday. The game also saw a double presentation. Firstly Town received the 'Charter Standard Club' award and then presented Cleator Moor with a memento to mark Cleator Moor's centenary year.

And so it was to Jarrow, finally, for the quarter final tie on the 13th. With illness, injury and Nathan Cook's suspension, such were Town's problems at this point that Mitch Cook was a named substitute, confirming what many people had believed for a while, he was itching to play, despite mentioning his knees quite a lot. Cook wasn't needed however, as Town convincingly beat their Tyneside opponents for the third time of the season. It took until the second half to break the deadlock when Joel Ramm fired home. Jarrow then shot themselves in the foot, ended the game with 9 men, and Town scored two more, Billy Logan's injury time deflected effort his first for the club, and another Josh Greening penalty. What Jarrow didn't need to do was self implode, but did in style, the first red card being a second yellow for a shove on Greening as he tried to get up after the awarding of the penalty, the second red also for a second yellow, this time for kicking the ball away after protesting – for a Jarrow goal kick after the referee awarded a Jarrow throw. Three games against

Jarrow, 14 scored, 1 conceded – a job well done, and perhaps more importantly, the game was finally out of the way!

The following Tuesday saw shockwaves sent through the Northern Under 19 Youth Alliance as the Academy side were beaten. Landlords Pickering were the victors in the League Cup quarter final. Joe Danby had scored twice for the under 19s, but it was too little too late, as at the time they were already 3 goals down. The double had gone. It was nights like these though that, perversely, the management didn't mind too much – of course they hated losing, especially in the cup and especially in a local derby, but they learnt far much more about the team than they had the previous games.

For the lads needing to bounce back from the under 19s disappointment, they could thank the Wearside Leagues fixture planner, as a trip to Guisborough was most kind. Sitting fourth bottom with one win in their last seven, against basement side Willington, it was a game Town would expect to win handsomely. It wasn't pretty but Town did the job, two late goals, meaning the game would finish 5-0. Carl Cook, who majestically stroked home that spot kick to win the shootout against Annfield Plain back in September, missed the chance to become the 19th different Town player to hit the net as he screwed a penalty past the post. Town were helped by Guisborough ending the game with just 9 men – the two red cards contributing well to Guisborough's total of 9 throughout the season. Wolviston were next up at Pindar and, as usual, Town expected 3 points despite the loss of three players. Danny Jenkinson had left Scarborough for a career in the Navy and Matt Perry and Ricky Ossai headed to the USA for football coaching jobs. Despite the tough solitary goal victory at Metcalfe Park earlier in the season, Wolviston arrived with a record pretty similar to that of Guisborough's – one win in nine, against Willington. It became a great day for Town. The game was over as a contest after ten minutes. Town were 3-0 up by this point, Josh Greening had grabbed a hat trick – his 17th in 16 games. Town didn't take their foot of the gas though and as usual, with home advantage, the surface they wanted and the majority of the 88 crowd behind them, they pummelled their opposition into submission. Joe Danby completed the scoring one minute from time with Town's eighth of the afternoon, and Robbie Hawkes came off the bench to hit the net for the first time since returning from injury, and Town had their biggest victory of the season so far. The attendance however was Town's lowest of the season, and the fourth lowest ever, proving that many more factors were at play than just results on the pitch.

The answer to what was Scarborough FC's first ever floodlit match is open to debate – Lord Londesborough paid for the clubs first game on October 2, 1879 to be played under the power of four 5000 candle-power lights under the rules of rugby football, and Boston United visited the Athletic Ground in September 1970 for what was billed as Scarborough's first floodlit home game. However, much clearer cut, the 24th March, 2010 was due to be Scarborough Town's. In an attempt to begin to clear the backlog of games, at some expense, GPCSC were hiring portable floodlights, for what was essentially an innovative experiment. The lights weren't quite 'conventional' being of a retractable nature – and New Marske didn't really fancy it – well after the North Riding Senior Cup show in October, they didn't fancy it then either. The referee did though and said the match was to go ahead. The lights were fine, lit the pitch up enough, and as such the game was on. It had taken all day to get the lights ready – 8 towers, one by one had been pushed, pulled and towed into place. The occasion was grand, although no attendance was finalised it was estimated at over 300, so of course, one of the lights failed. The referee apologetically said the game couldn't go ahead unless it worked, and the latest the game could start was 8pm – half an hour after the scheduled start. By 8.01pm, New Marske were in the bar, watching the evening's other scores roll in. By ten past eight, the lights were back on, but it was too late. Abandoned – the plucky experiment had failed – and didn't Town know about it – the officials still needed paying, and the internet messageboards went into overdrive. Rather than realising that the best part of £1000 had voluntarily been parted with to get the game played by hiring the lights, it turned into a 'big time charlie' debate as the money was spent. The longer term idea was that alongside the fixed floodlights, the school was also interested in portable ones – which would allow them freedom of movement, to take them where they required for coaching, whether that be on site or elsewhere – and the Town game was used partly as an experiment for them – the ease they went up and down and could be turned on and off and manoeuvred about scrutinised as much as the output.

Lightning struck twice in two days as the Under 19s league tie Pickering was plunged into darkness also. Normal service had resumed, as the Academy side were leading with only minutes remaining when the game fell dark. Luckily this meant the result stood and moved the under 19s one step closer to retaining their league crown. Chinese whispers suggested that the Asian betting syndicates that had caused such occurrences at West Ham United and Wimbledon in late 1997 may have had significant money on Scarborough Town Under 19s 3-1 Pickering Town Under 19s, but no further investigation was ever brought forward.

The Sunderland Shipowners Cup Semi Final followed, with a trip to New Marske, the first of four more meetings the sides would have before the end of the season. After returning home from Pindar shellshocked in the North Riding Senior Cup, New Marske had steadily climbed the table and had won 7 of their last 8. Add in the frostiness that had developed following New Marske's insistence that they would not be playing under the Pindar floodlights and it had the makings of tough battle. The game would not be over by half time as it had been before. This was mainly as Town hit 5 goals in the second half instead of the first, leaving a rather one sided semi final 6-1, and Town in their first cup final.

April 2010

As the intense run of games began to pick up pace, a testament to just how good the Under 19 side had become was summed up by the delight of two men who had travelled with Pontefract Collieries Under 19 side for the league clash as they commented with some delight that Ponte had just recorded their best ever result against Scarborough Academy – an 8-2 defeat, a better result than their previous 10-2, 10-3 and 12-0 defeats! The under 19 crown was firmly staying in Scarborough, as none of the chasing pack could mount a sustained challenge to the Academy boys. 5 of side, Cook, Greening, Brown, Logan and Danby then figured for Town as they faced Houghton Town with a changed team, as Mitch Cook had one eye on the larger threat posed by third placed Teesside Athletic just two days later. Houghton came to Pindar on the back of improved form, with a record of 4 wins, 3 draws and a solitary defeat in their last 8 outings, scoring 14 and conceding 8. As the winter weather began to end Town recorded their highest crowd since October as 155 people were present to see Joel Ramm open the scoring on just 3 minutes and, two minutes later, Matty Brown rode a couple of tackles before finding Wayne Brooksby who picked his spot just inside the goalkeepers left hand post. Houghton registered their first shot on target on the stroke of half time, but by this time the game had turned into how much Town could increase their goal difference by as the scoreline stood at 7-0. Josh Greening had hit an 8 minute hat trick, taking 3 minutes longer than his treble against Wolviston two weeks previously. The second half saw Town conserve energy for the Teesside test, with three half time substitutions confirming this. Joe Danby and Greening scored in the second half as Town hit nine for the first time in the Wearside, the ninth being Town's 100th league goal of the season – in all of 23 games. In the lead up to the game, Houghton proclaimed they had a secret weapon that they were ready to unleash on Scarborough. They wanted the win for

Ryhope, which probably just made the result more embarrassing. Most teams didn't big up their chances before visiting Pindar.

Town's assault on the title gained even more momentum just two days later as the championship race was effectively down to just two teams. Rob Clark, Georgie Rose and Neil Waterfield retook their places in the staring eleven for the visit of Teesside Athletic. Only Town had conceded fewer goals than the Teessiders who, unlike previous visitors Houghton, arrived at Pindar in their worst form of the season with two straight defeats without scoring against Easington Colliery (0-1) and Windscale (0-3) respectively. At half time, the game was finely poised. Town had, as was becoming the norm, raced into an early lead, with Georgie Rose reacting first to poke the ball into the net after his initial shot had crashed back off the crossbar. A wide free kick from Greening then evaded everyone including the keeper to put Town 2-0 up on 34 minutes, but another free kick pegged Town back ten minutes later as Jamie Clarke, who had spent the last two seasons as Northern League Spennymoor Town's leading scorer, smashed the ball through the wall and past an unsighted Rob Clark. After the 2-1 victory back in December, and 90 minutes two days earlier, Town could have been forgiven for holding out for the same result, but Town didn't do holding out. With a team talk ringing in their ears – they had now had 90 minutes without really hitting top gear - after the second half of Houghton and the first 45. So, they responded by upping the tempo and reached the 50th minute 4-1 up, the fourth being Wayne Brooksby with a cheeky near post finish when everyone, keeper included, was waiting for the ball to be angled towards the back post. Clarke became yet another opposition player to see red against Town when he received his second yellow with 15 minutes remaining, and after that Town pressed home the advantage, with Dean Craig firing home from the edge of the box before Matty Brown and Nathan Cook both finished one on one chances to conclude a thumping 7-1 victory and take the goal difference to a modest +87.

Effectively, barring a collapse, Town had promotion in the bag. Now 12 points clear of Teesside, with a game in hand, Town were close to achieving one of the main objectives of the season – earning the right to play at a higher level yet again. Ryhope didn't want promotion. Their facilities were not good enough, and the club were not about to improve them. This meant that second place was good enough if Town didn't win the league, of course, facilities pending. Just two days later came one of the games of the season as New Marske headed down for the rearranged league game. With a 6.30 start to beat the darkness, 163 people witnessed a topsy-turvy game with a skill level that easily could have graced a higher level. Well, New Marske were able to field a team with a few changes from that which had played Town two Saturdays ago, as Northern League Guisborough Town were without a game that evening, and some players were dual registered between the two clubs. Wayne Brooksby gave Town a slender half time lead, which was cancelled out with 15 minutes to go by visiting skipper Phillip Peggs, silencing the vocal Town backing temporarily. With his finger on his lips, Peggs ran the length of the touchline in celebration, which ironically was responsible for turning the volume up. Two yellow cards later, and New Marske were down to ten – but the dismissed Dan Wilkinson was not about to go quietly. The referee was influenced by the crowd apparently - influenced by the crowd, who had been influenced by a yellow card tackle by a player who had already been booked. He left the field, but stood outside the pitch surrounds watching the game, until the influencing home crowd made the referee aware of this, who halted the game until he disappeared to the changing rooms. On the pitch, time was running out, the robust New Marske back 9 seemingly impossible to break down. They understood by playing deep, one of Town's biggest assests – speed - became harder to use, as there was no space to use it. From the two games so far, they had done their homework well. But they missed something crucial. Town packed the box for a corner, so Marske packed it with them, confident that if they could stop Neil Waterfield winning the header, they would be able to clear it. Not quite, as it was only cleared to the edge of the box, met by Georgie Rose, to slam emphatically home past an unsighted Justin Hutchinson. Cue mass hysteria. One minute later, it was mass hysteria mark II. Another corner saw the ball go straight to Mark Barber on the edge of the box, who slammed home himself. Not quite as exquisite as the cup semi final, but receiving much more acclaim. Marske left the field broken, a lot of energy expended and nothing whatsoever to show for it. With several Northern League players faced and beaten, the future looked bright for the boys from Scarborough.

Next up was New Marske, seriously, again. This time it was the League Cup semi final, but without the luck of Wednesday, a Marske goal in each half was enough to see off Town, who huffed and puffed, came close, but only had a late consolation from Billy Logan to cheer. After 10 straight victories, Town had come undone, as had Ryhope, who also fell in their semi final to Easington, meaning the top two wouldn't dominate everything on offer this season. Another two days later was another game, Town's fifth in ten days. Away at Teesside, this was the cup final dress rehearsal, and with another 11 games to play in a month and three days, losing two in a row could spell disaster to lose belief, or to begin to doubt your own ability at this stage of the season. With a stiff breeze from the North Sea, despite playing now inside the enclosed ground rather than outside as Town had done on their last trip to Redcar for their ever first competitive game, Town fell behind early on, but not for long, as luckily Dean Craig ventured forward and slammed home after 13 minutes. With Town up against a Teesside side intent on sending a message out after the 7-1 mauling at Pindar, the game ebbed and flowed, with neither side staying on top for long. The bar saved Town in injury time, and preserved Town's ever growing unbeaten League run, with what was a useful point. But Ryhope had defeated Cleator Moor Celtic by a solitary goal, extending their lead to 8 points. Town had 3 games in hand, but now, there was no room for error. Only 3 of the last ten league games would be at home - one of those being Ryhope themselves, and the other two being top 6 sides, Easington, who had defeated Town previously, and Annfield Plain, who had took Town to penalties and only lost by a single goal in the August league meeting.

Cameron Dobson pulled on a Town shirt for the first time at Hartlepool. In local league football, Dobson was scoring for fun – he had been training with Town for a while, and so with the games mounting up, it was time to introduce him. What would turn out to be a silver lining about so many games in such a short period of time was simply that there was no time to dwell on anything. Having a week to put right a bad result just increased the pressure, but when it was game after game, a week was a long time – it was 3 or 4 games at the moment. Despite briefly being one goal all mid way through the first half, Town ran out 4-1 winners. So now, 8 points behind, 3 games in hand and the small matter of a cup final. It was due to be one hell of an end to the season.

Town travelled into County Durham the next Saturday to the small village of Coxhoe, to play at one of the most picturesque grounds in the league. Overlooking the countryside and with Durham cathedral peeking into the skyline in the distance, Beechfield Park offers extensive views and is a most pleasant place to spend an afternoon. Offering ladies at half the price of men, with covered seating in three different areas, one complete with padded benches, it is a ground to visit again and again. Town probably wished they could too. There was no such scare which had led to the unbelievably late show way back in September, as two early goals from Joel Ramm and Jamie Patterson calmed Town. Luke Jenkinson then proceeded to hit his fouth hat trick in a Town shirt, as Town ran out 6-2 victors and seemed to be back on track, and not suffering from fatigue.

Ashbrooke on a Wednesday night does not have the same appeal as a sunny Saturday at Coxhoe. In the middle of a Sunderland suburban housing estate, Town had already visited the ground back in October, and struggled their way to a 2-0 victory over Silksworth, with whom Belford House share the ground. The pitch in October had been poor – so after a wet and cold winter, Towns passing style could prove difficult to play. The assembled crowd was a mix – a few Ashbrooke followers and locals dispersed between those who had made the trip from Scarborough and a decent amount of those from nearby Ryhope – Ashbrooke supporters for the night. After a cagey opening, it was the Ashbrooke/Ryhope contingent who cheered first, as they took the lead and held it until half time. Up popped Joel Ramm to flick his header over the keeper and level proceedings with 5 miuntes to go. Injury time saw Cameron Dobson screw wide from a good chance and Town had been held. Advantage Ryhope. Unhappy with the referee, Nathan Cook told him his opinion of his performance, and to his horror was shown red for the second time of the season. Mitch Cook was understandably furious, and told his son so. What he didn't need also was Ryhope/Ashbrooke/Locals goading him as he left the pitch. Told they were unwelcome in Ashbrooke, Town's followers were gruffly told to get out while they could or they might have their cars smashed up. Lovely place, lovely club. A bizarre set of events were occurring at Pickering, where the under 19s were facing Pocklington on the same evening. Without any of the under 19s who played first team football, it was a great chance for the younger (still) lads to begin their under 19 alliance journeys. A 4-2 victory meant the future looked bright – in a couple of years Town could have another set of youngsters ready to make the step up – this was team comprised of 16 and 17 year olds, who had beaten an under 19 side, without much experience of playing at the level. Another testament, to the way they had been schooled to play the game.

With the first team needing to respond after dropping points, it was time to go to Ryhope's other best friends, Houghton Town. Once more, what had happened at Pindar would be irrelevant, as the night time away trips meant the players would arrive, in some cases, minutes before kick off. To ease the crisis, Liam Salt had agreed to join to a dual registered basis from Pickering Town. Salt was a former Scarborough FC Centre of Excellence striker, who was at the club for over 5 years. After failing to make the grade at Boro when they were a professional outfit, he had returned to local football and Pickering. The followers expecting a Wembley like surface at Leyburn Grove would be left bitterly disappointed, but the pain was somewhat eased with the gate being open and no one charging admission giving a free evening. With a player crisis themselves, Houghton were ready for the season to end, and were nearly there – with just one more to play after this – unlike Town's seven! Manager Steve Patton had pulled on the gloves for the home side, and through bravery, luck and some awful finishing and composure, the home side got to half time goalless, a far cry from the opening 45 minutes at Pindar. Unable to damage Houghton, Town turned to the bench. Enter

Robbie Hawkes, within 5 minutes of his entrance he had broke the resistance. Nathan Cook bravely had won the ball, charged through the middle and fed Hawkes, who shaved the underside of the crossbar as he put Town in front from 18 yards. After playing for what seemed like an age with a nervous one goal cushion, when Town didn't know whether to continue charging forward for a second, or unfamiliarly defend a one goal lead, another substitute Joe Danby, sealed the points. The nature of the win was what was impressive, many teams by now has seen the way to stop Town was by constantly breaking up the flow of the game. But Town had doggedly persevered and been rewarded. Five miles down the road came the news of the night. Ryhope had squandered a two goal lead and had ended up drawing with Town's local neighbours Kirkbymoorside. With two games in hand, the gap was back to 5 points.

There was a score to settle as Easington Colliery visited Town. Having ended Town's unbeaten start to the season and inflicted one of only two league defeats, Town wanted revenge. With the title race having swung in their direction also, Town didn't want to and couldn't afford to slip up again. The crowd grew again to 167, as Town had a home game for the first time in two and a half weeks. Both sides tried to start brightly, playing attacking football, refreshingly without a foul or infringement in sight. Rob Clark and his opposite number James Winter were both playing for a well deserved clean sheet, taking it in turns to thwart their opponent. Easington pressed, Clark saved, and Winter, almost sweeping on the edge of the centre circle, sportingly applauded and voiced his approval to his Town equivalent. The game was set for a goalless draw – similar by result and circumstance to the 0-0 draw with Norton and Stockton Reserves the season previously as Town chased the title. Enter Robbie Hawkes (part two). After being thwarted for 20 minutes since his arrival on the pitch, and struggling to make an impact, Hawkes cut inside his man 20 yards out nearing the left hand side of penalty box and let fly. The only part of Winter that moved was his jaw, as it dropped in horror. 87 minutes, 1-0. Easington, though shell-shocked attacked from kick off, but lost possession, Hawkes ran, the ball glued to his toes, and headed directly for the goal this time down the right. 15 yards out he hit the same top corner again. 88 minutes 2-0. Town had claimed a big three points, and the two goal victory had enhanced their goal difference to +100, with 126 league goals scored and just 26 conceded in 31 matches. Still second with two games in hand, but only two points behind. Town had dealt with the pressure, Ryhope hadn't. They had lost away at Annfield Plain, by 1 goal to nil. The clubhouse was ecstatic. After watching two teams play football in the right way for 90 minutes, with two brilliant goals, the news was the icing on the cake. The belief grew even more. The only word of caution was that by beating Ryhope this put the Plain 23 league games unbeaten, and they were coming to Pindar next Saturday. Town had two more away games before then – and one of them was New Marske.

Another warm sunny evening greeted Town as they arrived in Boldon. With Ryhope's form taking a turn for the worst, and them playing 3rd placed Teesside Athletic tonight, the mood in the team was buoyant. Cook rotated the team again, with Joe Danby and Matthew Brown both getting starts. Adjacent to Northern League side Jarrow Roofing Boldon Community Association, Boldon themselves have dreams of reaching the Northern League one day. With a tidy ground and floodlight poles in place (and floodlights by the time you are reading this) the major stumbling block to the plans are the on the field performances. As usual with a visit from Town, Boldon produced a programme for the Town's paper chasers. At £2 it was not only the most expensive but also the same price as admission!

It took less than a minute for Town to open the scoring, and when the second was added inside ten minutes, the home keepers grandfather, who had predicted a Town landslide victory pre match, although perhaps worried about what his grandson was facing, seemed content and sure that he would be proved right. It took a little longer for the third, but after much overplaying and trying to emulate Arsenal by walking the ball over the line, Matty Brown took full advantage of his opportunity to finish the third. Half time gave an opportunity for those who had taken enough pound coins to read the programme to pass the time, and after a thorough read of the four sides of A4, the other 14 minutes passed quickly. With the game safe after a fourth on 54 minutes courtesy of an own goal, another triple substitution followed to rest players for two days time at Marske. Liam Gildea's return for his first appearance since Kirkbymoorside away in August was massively overshadowed by an elderly gentleman in a fetching blue coat who was unhappy. What he was unhappy at wasn't entirely obvious, but he proceeded to get through the pitch surrounds and confront Mitch Cook face to face in the away dugout. As Cook sidestepped to ignore him and continue instructing and watching Town, the assistant offered advice that it would be unwise for him to lay a hand on the intruder, then afterwards signalled the referee, who in turn asked for help from the Boldon dugout to remove the man. By this point, the two dugouts were not on speaking terms and the home dugout especially didn't want to aid the referee unnecessarily. Whilst this was occurring, Cook proceeded to anger the man further with the help of his substituted players by ignoring him further and whistling every time he attempted to speak to him. It took time, but the blue coat was escorted away, by which I mean behind the barrier to be directly next to the away dugout instead, and the game drew to a conclusion with a most comfortable 4-0 victory. Ryhope still had fight however, the last two results had hurt them, and they clicked to take it out on Teesside with a 3-0 victory, increasing the pressure on Wednesday nights games, when both teams would face the two teams who had dumped them out of the League Cup. The Ryhope result did have a silver lining for Town though, as it guaranteed them second place, and with Ryhope not having applied to move up, that meant promotion!

So, for the fifth and final time of the season, Town faced New Marske. The huge run of night time kick offs had taken its toll, and Town struggled for players, as employers simply couldn't grant time off work every other night. Another Scarborian, Wayne Aziz made his debut, like Liam Salt, Aziz also played for Pickering Town and had joined on a dual registered purpose, with the purpose of being around on the odd night when the games caught up. Despite the hugely disjointed side, and with a back four who did not play together regularly, Town took an early lead through Josh Greening. Aziz's Town career lasted just 39 minutes as a pulled hamstring forced him off and ended his season, but by that time Town were chasing the game at 2-1 down, the second goal seeing New Marske's dual registered Sam Garvie, who regularly tormented Northern League Division 1 sides for Shildon, scoring from the spot after being fouled himself. After the break, Joe Danby was brought down and Nathan Cook restored parity and once more Town's manner irritated their opponents to the point of no return – this time it was Andy Futcher who saw red after a tirade of abuse to the man in black. From this point on Town poured forward, looking for a winner, but were thwarted. A point away at New Marske was a good one – but a Ryhope win would really up the pressure, their lead extending to 5 points – Town with three to play, Ryhope just the one – against Town. But it hadn't been as simple as that for Ryhope – Town's point began to look even better as news filtered its way down the North East coast that James Winter had inspired Easington again – they had beaten Ryhope 1-0. There was now only one point between the two, and Town still had two games in hand as the most gruelling April possible ended. Town had played 12 games in April, 8 of them away from home and 6 of these had been night games. As important as everything which had happened on the pitch during April, off the pitch, significant progress had been made also; The college had two planning applications entered with the Borough Council, one for eight floodlight towers around the pitch, next to the existing floodlit astroturf, the other for a metre and a half on hard standing around the football pitch – which essentially provided disabled access to the facility, and the construction of new hard outdoor tennis courts, to aid the development of Scarborough Tennis Club, who were also part of the Pindar sporting community. At this time, the college were in further negotiation with a developer to improve other sports facilities further – to make the college home to a dedicated sports village, including a golf driving range and centre and equestrian facilities, as part of a deal which would see the school receive more land in exchange for allowing an access road through land they owned away from the main school site. The applications now had a 21 day consultation period. It seemed the long standing wrangles were drawing to a close – soon the future would be clear.

May 2010

With Ryhope only having Town to face the following Saturday, anticipation was high for the visit of Annfield Plain. A point or more would take Town top of the league for the first time since the Kirkbymoorside show at Pindar back at the end of October. Sensing this anticipation, 191 spectators headed to Pindar, as the gate increased for the 5th time in 6 games. With an almost full side available, fortress Pindar once again lived up to its reputation. Four unanswered goals, including another two from Greening, and Town were top. Plain had been unbeaten in the league since mid September until this point. After two extremely tough games previously against the Plain, it was a measure of Town's improvement over the season.

Teesside Athletic had home advantage for the Sunderland Shipowners Cup Final. A supporters bus travelled from Scarborough, and 'away' support made up a large contingent of the 245 strong crowd, with varying estimates all agreeing that over 100 had made the 45 mile journey. Mitch Cook made just one change from the side that had dispatched Annfield Plain just two days previously, seemingly not worried about this game marking Town's 14th game 30 days! As with the previous trip just 21 days (but 9 matches!) ago, the wind blew across the ground from goalmouth to goalmouth, with Town playing into the wind in the first half. It was white shirts and blue shorts for Town, as after bringing their home strip, it was too similar to the Teessider's red and blue shirts, meaning that Town had to wear the home sides change strip. The 7-1 at Pindar was long forgotten – the draw in the return fixture had shown that Teesside had learnt, and were not about to let Town play when they could help it, after an even opening, it was the home side who took the lead, with Dale Mendum on the end of a flowing passing move Town supporters were used to seeing at the other end. But Town hadn't made the final to lose at the last hurdle, and responded within ten minutes. Wayne Brooksby, as usual, who spent all afternoon terrorising his opposite full backs, hit the bar and Josh Greening, as usual, was on hand to level things up. Brooksby then slotted Town in front after the hour, and Town missed opportunities to close the game out before being hit on the counter attack, which ended in Mendum heading home for 2-2. Four good quality goals – this was certainly a cup final. As Town pressed for the winner they deserved on their second half display, Matty Brown's strike was safely tipped over the bar by the goalkeeper. From the resulting corner, after encouragement from the dugout to test the keeper, Josh Greening whipped the ball into the danger area, alluding everyone including the goalkeeper and the player on the far post to nestle above him in the top corner and give Town the advantage once more at 3-2. Greening could only go to one place to celebrate, and ran to the bench, ending in Mitch Cook's arms. Playing against the wind, Teesside couldn't get back into the game, and it was Town who could have hit the net again, but had done enough. The whistle sounded, the white shirts were off and the red and black stripes were on for the presentation. Georgie Rose lifted the Shipowners Cup, with cautious excitement due to a culmination of it being rather large and Rose not being the tallest, and Town had completed half of the double. The celebrations saw a release of months of expectation, months of being kicked and finally they saw the rewards – and the celebrations could be twice as big if everything went right in six days time.

It couldn't have been any clearer for the visit of Ryhope to Pindar. If Town could avoid defeat they would be Wearside League champions in their first season at the level, and would complete the double. Defeat would give Ryhope a one point advantage, having completed their season and leave Town needing at least a point from the long final day trip to Cumbria to face Cleator Moor Celtic to take the title on goal difference. With a full five days rest behind them, Town were recharged – it was their biggest rest period in a month – the month being 14 games long. Ryhope's break had been longer – it had been ten days since their defeat to Easington, so they would be chomping at the bit to end their season on a high, and to make Town need to play in Cumbria. As in recent weeks, a larger than average crowd was expected at Pindar. As such, the game took extra importance off the pitch. After what seemed to be a negative campaign against Pindar hosting football, this was an opportunity to show how it could deal with crowds, expected to be far larger than Town's average. The matchday operation was like never before. A tunnel, or 'safe walkway' for the players and officials was roped off leading them to the pitch and the PA system was used to create that craved for matchday experience. The Sunderland Shipowners Cup, with its red and black ribbons fluttering in the breeze, was on proud display on a table next to the pay booth. Those taking admission were under strict instruction not to let it out of their sight! The cup itself, with the names of Sunderland and Middlesbrough amongst others, was engraved '2009/10 Teesside Athletic' as Town had lifted the trophy. Was this a mistake from the previous year when Teesside Athletic had captured the cup at League Champions Newton Aycliffe? Or perhaps the cup just hadn't gone where planned!

By kick off at 2.30, a new record attendance again was set, with a relatively massive 428 spectators entering Pindar– almost double the previous record set back in August. This was two thirds the crowd that Scarborough FC had recorded for a Conference North game in their final season. The hearts and minds campaign was working.

As typical with hyped up 'big' games, on the pitch was a scrappy affair with little incident. The first half passed anonymously, with little between the sides. So did halftime, as 'ballgate' seemed a distant memory. Town were 45 minutes from the title, all they had to do was shut Ryhope out. But Town being Town never played for a draw, and never held back from tearing forward at every occasion. A second yellow card greeted Ryhope's Richard Jordon on the hour mark. Sensing their opportunity, Town pressed and after 73 minutes Josh Greening swept in Robbie Hawkes low cross at the back post to the delight of the 400 home 'fans'. As he ran to the corner flag to celebrate, any chance of a calm, collected, cool celebration went out the window and he found himself on the bottom of an 11 man pile up – yes, 11, Rob Clark beat his personal best and ran the full 100 yards to join the group. The seconds counted down, and after it seemed like the referees watch had gone backwards for 5 minutes, he blew. Town were jubilant, Ryhope despondent. The whistle signified the second successive season of a treble for the club, as the first team completed its so sought after double. The Wearside League chairman outshone his Teesside League equivalent, as he was in attendance to present the trophy. There was a hush as the majority stayed behind. Ryhope received their runners up medals to polite applause and conducted themselves well in what must have been a horrible occasion. They gave their congratulations to Town, and disappeared to their dressing room, not wishing to see what was about to happen. The trophy was presented, and unlike Mr Blatter likes to, the chairman didn't remain amongst the celebration's, which just left Georgie Rose, now well practised, to lift the League Championship to a roar of approval from fans, followers, family and friends.

The clubhouse was filled with well wishers and people basking in the glory of what had been achieved. Ryhope were presented with champagne, to congratulate them on their season –capturing the Monkwearmouth Charity Cup and the second placed finish representing one of their most successful seasons since their truly golden age of the 1960s, and to be an offering to mend the ever so frosty atmosphere between the two clubs after being locked so tightly in the title battle, and the November meeting. The well deserved celebrations continued long into the night and, as always, the champagne tasted that little bit nicer when drunk from the silverware.

There was a milestone for the under 19s still to come, as four days after the jubilation of the senior side, the longer, light filled evenings allowed a home game in Scarborough at Pindar, for the first time in three years and one month, since Bridlington Town had visited the McCain Stadium. The game against Garforth finished goalless, as the Under 19s continued to plan for the next season, and played without those who would be too old. The season had ended, making it two full league programmes without defeat.

The season finished at Cleator Moor Celtic, and Town did exactly what they had done on their last trip to Cumbria, drew 3-3 after being both 2-0 and 3-1 up. Carl Cook scored without a doubt own goal of the season, as he chipped Rob Clark from all of 25 yards, and Matty Brown scored in his final appearance for the club before jetting off to begin a new life at College in the USA. The Cleator Moor programme editor commented on Town, with his introduction reading *'They have been, in my humble opinion, the best and most entertaining team in the league this season. Their brand of football is a treat to watch, even if at times if you are in the opposition camp'*. The curtain was down on the first season at step 7; Town had come an awfully long way. But it had worked, there was no doubt the players had developed. Scarborough had a group of its own players ready to grace a higher level again. Cumbria disappeared as the bus headed east, for an end of season celebration in Newcastle.

Presentation evening saw Carl Cook rewarded for his consistency across his 43 appearances with the coveted player of the season award. Mark Barber took the Scarborough Evening News' equivalent, and Matty Brown took the under 19 version. Josh Greening took the top goalscorer awards for both the first team and the under 19's, with Robbie Hawkes being victorious in the 'goal of the season' poll for his goal that broke the deadlock against Easington, though how everyone remembered all 190 goals when voting is beyond me!

As previously mentioned the aim of this book is not to place blame, throw accusations or point the finger. It is a celebration of two brilliant years, two years which it would seem unimaginable to put the word 'brilliant' to after being used to watching League and Conference football in nice, warm stadia, played by professionals and the highest level of semi professionals. What follows has been pieced together to offer the story of summer 2010.

At a point where Town needed improved facilities to be able to compete at the level they deserved, as previously mentioned, opposition became rife. Despite the club offering local young players the chance to showcase their talent, some residents local to GPCSC vociferously voiced their opposition. It transpired they weren't alone in their objections – Sport England also objected, on the basis that a metre wide path around the existing concrete post fence, and the 'footprint' that 8 floodlight towers would leave constituted a loss of playing field space. Whatever the objection, the college worked hard to meet it, revising and amending the application on numerous occasions. But every time they did, the basis of the objection changed. The objection included the loss of a cricket wicket – that being the one which had been relocated to another of the schools playing fields over two years ago – it seemed old ariel photographs were all that Sport England were basing their objection on!

There was big news days later, as the FA's League Committee decided that despite Town winning the feeder league for the Northern League (a league that Scarborough FC had also spent seasons in) that for geographical reasons, if Town were to play at step 6, it would have to be in the North East Counties League. It would be the NCEL's decision to accept Town though, with the main stumbling block being the ground situation. It was in Scarborough that the big decision was to be made. At the Grand Hotel, a hotel with football decision making history, having in the past hosted the FA's summer conference. It was similar to that of the Wearside the year before – a presentation, then leave the room for the other sides to consider what they had heard, and back in to hear the fate. It all came down to the ground assurances – something that it was going to be hard to give. With no planning permission, and nearly a month until a decision was due, whatever the call was going to be it was going to be viewed somewhere by someone as 'dodgy'. Letting Town in was letting a club without planning permission for the requisite floodlights in, not letting them in meant if planning permission was granted then the step 7 winners had been inexplicably declined a step 6 place. Some big clubs in the decision supported Town, some were more sceptical. Town were examined thoroughly, from finances to the ground and the future. A decision had been reached. Scarborough Town were accepted to the North East Counties League Division 1. But it was provisional – it was on the basis that Town would be granted planning permission. Floodlights were needed to start the season, and hard standing and cover would be needed by March 31 the following year. Floodlights – 8 poles, stood between the development continuing and the end of the road.

The elation began to sour as the anxious wait for planning permission continued. The FA introduced a measure which stunted the club's youth development, without seemingly there being too much reason for the move. The FA Youth cup, the flagship of youth football, the benchmark, was now out of reach. The new ruling was that only youth teams could be entered by a club which had entered the FA Cup, Trophy or Vase the previous season, which of course Town hadn't. To rub it in further, Town hadn't been accepted to the FA Vase for the coming season, as the ground grading deadline was much earlier than Town's ground had been acceptable, meaning that it was a minimum of two seasons before the Academies finest would be able to test themselves on a national scale.

As with the previous seasons, things started to hot up when the fixtures were released. As usual, Town would be playing away to begin with, to give the maximum amount of time after (or if) the go-ahead was given for the hard standing and floodlights. As with the previous season also, it would be a long trip first up, with a trip to Shirebrook Town of Mansfield, followed by Scunthorpe based Appleby Frodingham, who the under 19s had confidently dispatched the youth team of in the past. Rossington Main of the Doncaster area would be next up and finally the first home game was when AFC Emley would come to Town at the end of August.

The 8th of July should have been significant as it was the day Scarborough Borough Council had deemed 'Target Determination Day' for the planning application, but it came and passed without an announcement, or even a footnote. Town pressed on, making arrangements for the coming season ready for NCEL football – it was all that could be done. Liaison work was almost daily at this point, with meetings and dialogue between GPCSC, the FA, Sport England and planning officers – but talk was just that – and unless it meant a written guarantee, the future was looking very murky. The prices were to rise, in line with League policy – up to a whopping £3 for adults. With overhead costs expected to similar to last season – the Wearside and NCEL both had a combined mileage which wasn't massively dissimilar, an extra £1 brought in per adult was useful – people would be more than happy to pay it, yet the difference to the club could be significant over the course of the season.

The next week saw the problems come to a head, and it looked like the admission charge was going to be completely irrelevant. The Council didn't hear the planning application. They said it was going to be at least August. That meant no guarantee by the deadline day – which it seemed meant no place in the NCEL. Town had acceptable plans in place for temporary hard standing and cover, and only had two home evening games before Christmas scheduled – more thoughts circulated – could they just be switched to give more time? Could just two games be played elsewhere? But the fact of the matter was the offer of membership was dependent upon an accepted planning application. The league responded in the only way it could, issuing the following statement:-

"Scarborough Town was admitted to the League on a provisional basis at last month's AGM.
"The provisional membership was subject to the club receiving planning permission from Scarborough Town Council for floodlights, hard-standing and covered accommodation at its current ground.
"To date, no such planning approval has been received and the offer of membership will be withdrawn on Wednesday 21st July, 2010, unless written planning approval is received from Scarborough Town Council for all the requirements and the club are able to do the specific work within the required timeframe should planning permission be received."

One of the key problems was that time had never been strictly enforced, which had left the club in limbo. The Borough Council's consultation documents had required a reply within 21 days from the 18th of May. That day passed, and it was almost a month later when Sport England objected further.
Light relief was provided two days before the day of reckoning in the most English way possible - a game of cricket. A select Town eleven faced local league side Cloughton. After fielding first and restricting their hosts to a modest 89 from their 20 overs, Town found an outlet for their frustration, and began to contemplate a new sport they could look to dominate. Billy Logan, with the most unorthodox

cricket Cloughton had ever seen continued the good work that openers, and keen cricketers, Joe Danby and Sean Exley had started. The whole team chipped in with runs, including Hugh Bellamy and Mitch Cook, and Town eased home.

Away from the cricket pitch, a last minute battle was taking place. Reusing the Athletic Ground was mooted, the club announced it had been encouraged by the Council to submit proposals, and that its restoration figures were much lower than the Council's previously indicated ones. But of course, this would take longer than a fortnight to sort out, and still required approval for the floodlights in the short term. Groundsharing in order to gain promotion was a no-no – that was well known. Had Town played regularly elsewhere, it wouldn't have been a problem, but of course, this was about Scarborough. Whitby Town was an option – Town had groundshared there in the past for the North Riding Senior Cup, and were accommodated to the extent of the Whitby Town chairman becoming involved to speak to the FA and NCEL to offer the Turnbull Ground as Town's temporary home. The NCEL would only accept this, if it was on a temporary basis – temporary being 13 weeks. The 13 weeks, came from further council discussions – positive noises had been made that if the planning applications were withdrawn, then re entered on a 'temporary' basis – i.e. until the new Sports Village the council had promised to build was ready, then success was likely. The hearing of the application though, wouldn't be until August. So, with deadline just two days away now, the guarantee was far from concrete – the two days passed – and without the needed guarantee, the inevitable happened, with the following statement being issued by the NCEL:-

"The KoolSport Northern Counties East League wishes to announce that it has withdrawn the provisional offer of membership granted to Scarborough Town FC at its AGM on 12th June, 2010.
This withdrawal is due to the Club not receiving planning permission for floodlights, hard-standing and spectator covered accommodation which are all requirements to enable full League membership to be achieved."

By having to resign from the Wearside League in order to accept promotion, Town were in limbo. They would not have the facilities to play at Step 6, but they no longer had a place at Step 7, and it transpired after a meeting of Wearside clubs, a vote went against Town rejoining by 19 votes to 1. Other football clubs got to decide Town's fate. It looked as if the only football Town would be able to champion for the forthcoming season was the under 19s. But a decision was made on the immediate future – the players needed to find new clubs, so the two friendlies arranged against higher ranked opposition would go ahead. It would be a chance to showcase what Town had achieved, and almost as a cattle market, allowing other clubs to watch and see what they fancied.

Marske United's home, Mount Pleasant staged Town's penultimate game. Marske had finished 4th in the Step 6 Northern League second division, and surely would have sealed promotion, had they not also had a hugely impressive run to the last 8 of the FA Vase. Dean Craig and Joel Ramm had already accepted offers to ply their trade at Step 5 for Pickering Town, but Town still had the majority of team together. Town began looking short on match practise, as they were, whilst the home side were playing their fourth friendly already. The game was tidy, and as the half wore on, both teams were confident in the manner they played, and were pleasing on the eye. The opener came with 8 minutes until the break, as Rob Clark dropped a routine cross, leaving Marske striker Adam Gell with the simplest of finishes. Town began to fire in the second period however; Luke Jenkinson was felled leaving Nathan Cook to tuck away the resulting penalty. Within five minutes, Robbie Hawkes continued where he had left off the previous season, his dipping half volley beating the keeper, putting Town in front with 8 minutes left. Town couldn't quite hold on, as Danny Brunskill fired through a crowded box to give Marske a draw. What was evident though was that despite everything that had happened off the field, despite all the uncertainty, the Town lads just wanted to play football, and again they proved that they were good enough to compete at a higher level than they had previously had the chance.

One final twist was on the cards after the weekend though, with the resignation of South Bank St Peters from the Teesside League 1st Division, with their season a fortnight away from beginning. The FA suggested that perhaps Town could go back to what is 'unofficially' Step 8 and take over South Bank's fixtures. But the side was a development one – this would offer no development to any of the players who had played last season, and so it would mean starting again. The problem with this was that over half the under 19's had played Wearside football, and so this wouldn't benefit them – with the younger lads not eligible to play fist team football yet due to not being old enough, would Town be able to scrape a team together if this was the case? It would be 12 days until the Teesside League would make their decision – 12 Days that the club didn't have, for once, they wanted an early deadline.

If the future looked bleak before, it looked depressing next, as it transpired that the under 19s wouldn't be able to compete either. The league stated that every under 19 side had to be attached to a senior team competing in a recognised league, and that their deadline for informing them what League that was the last day of July – giving two days to sort out the future. Now of course, this wasn't a problem back in 2007, as Scarborough FC had folded and the Academy moved to Pindar, a senior or open age side was nothing but an idea – but the under 19s continued their membership regardless. The Teesside League weren't meeting until August 11, cue a frantic rush. It started with an appeal for a delay until the 11th – the FA asked the League – the League said no to the FA. At least we know where the power lies. Then a late switch was mooted using Scarborough Athletic's senior club registration – the under 19s would continue along the same path, just with a different registration number. But even this was blocked – despite the application being completed by the deadline; the league committee chose not to accept any Scarborough side.

With the certainty of no under 19 football, what had been looming concluded a couple of days before the Teesside League's meeting as a change in leadership at Pindar led to a change in the sporting outlook, as such they would have to re-enter into negotiations over the facilities – it was all too short notice for it – Town couldn't guarantee anything, so had to withdraw any application to the Teesside League. Game over.

And so, to Queensgate, Bridlington, where the Scarborough Town story winds down. Bridlington Town had won the Step 5 NCEL Premier Division last season, and had turned down promotion to the Evo-Stick league on financial grounds. Bridlington fielded two former Scarborough FC players, in goalkeeper Mark Wilberforce and left back Danny Brunton, Town were at full strength apart from the departed Ramm and Craig. The game was evenly matched, despite the league difference. Luke Jenkinson finished smartly to give Town a half time lead, but Craig Hogg, Bridlington's former Scarborough Athletic striker levelled shortly after half time as he finished neatly when through on goal. It was Nathan Cook who then made it happen. Picking up the ball in his own half, he surged. It was almost becoming a trademark. After riding tackles left, right and centre he had reached the penalty box. Sandwiched, he fell. He dusted himself off, adjusted his socks, and sent Wilberforce the wrong way. Bridlington looked for a way back into the game, but couldn't. A memorable victory was completed in the final minute as Wayne Brooksby, moved in from the touchline and curled the ball over the keeper into the far corner to have the honour of the first and last goals the team had scored. The full time whistle blew, and signified the ending of more than just the match.

People were committed to keeping Town going, to provide an outlet for local talent to be able to play at the highest level possible, and to give the opportunity for people to watch the highest level of football possible in the Town. But that was it for the team, for the story. The players needed to develop, to continue becoming as good as they can be, and for the first time, and through no fault of their ability they would have to split to achieve this.

As for the people who made this story, Wayne Brooksby headed to the Evo Stick Premier, with Hull based North Ferriby United. The Cook brothers along with Joe Danby and Mark Barber joined Bridlington Town, courtesy of an offer from Gary Allinson, the Bridlington manager who welcomed any Town players to Bridlington who wanted to train with them. Neil Waterfield went north, and signed for Northern League side Marske United. Robbie Hawkes joined Joel Ramm and Dean Craig at Pickering Town, but then left shortly after to join Scarborough Athletic of the same division.

But then there was a change. Mitch Cook was back in football, taking over at Pickering Town after Mark Wood's resignation after a difficult start to the season. Bob MacDonald continued his 20 year association with Mitch and followed. Georgie Rose, Rob Clark and Josh Greening joined, as did the four Bridlington players. Robbie Hawkes returned and Neil Waterfield came down. Darren Clough, Liam Salt and Wayne Aziz were already at the club, along with Mike McNaughton and Kevin Martin, both former Scarborough FC players. Wayne Brooksby singed dual registration forms along with Ged Dalton, also at Whitby Town, finally Matt Perry and Billy Logan signed. Under 19s players moved, the squad began to train as it had. At the time of writing, their debut season had just finished - the Pikes came home 7th - with just one defeat in their final ten matches, including a 5-0 victory over local rivals Scarborough Athletic. The production line looks set to continue, with the Under 19s set for the league runners up spot and another league cup final appearance. More academy players have tasted success, with Danny Glendenning, Tom Fenwick, Ali Homes and James Gunn all tasting first team football, and Josh Clayton achieving the same with Scarborough Athletic also.

The story splits in two ways – the manager and the players on a new chapter, continuing their development at a higher level for the third consecutive season, each one with a jump, from Step 9 to Step 7 and now Step 5. How high could a group of Scarborough lads, all who should get at least another ten good years in the game go? But it doesn't end quite for Scarborough Town either – the committee used the time off to prepare to re enter football in 2011/12. Mid November saw the club gain the 2010 Scarborough and District Sports Council Team of the Year for the league title which *'highlighted the abilities of our local footballers'*. At the time of writing, it is still league unknown, ground unknown, manager unknown and players unknown for next season. After summer 2010, until something is concrete, the town committee are reluctant to make it public now.

But their mantra remains the same – to provide senior competitive football for local lads.

Everyone who has ever played, watched or has an interest in football knows it can be a cruel, hurtful game – so the memories of the good times become even more priceless.

About The Author

Chris Daniel began watching Scarborough FC aged six, and was immediately hooked on his hometown side. With a strong interest in all things sporting, and as a postgraduate social historian at Durham University, he tries to marry to the two together in as much of his academic work as possible – culminating in a dissertation on Armed Services Football in Wartime. Currently he is working on the Origins of County Durham Football and its Relationship with Industry. In any free time this leaves, Chris is both a keen footballer and football coach throughout winter and a long distance runner over the summer. This is his first attempt at a book.